Future

Anterior

Future Anterior
Volume IV, Number 2
Winter 2007

1. Venturi and Rauch Architects, reconstruction of Benjamin Franklin's 1780s home, Philadelphia, 1976–78.
Photograph by author, 2003.

Preservation's Anonymous Lament

The ultimate form of cultural consecration for a preservationist is to be recognized as the one that changed the limits of what does and does not deserve to be preserved, culturally admired, and transmitted. The heretical challenger will always accuse the establishment of failing to operate by the established rule of preservation's *illusio* to bring life to the past. This was the technique used by James Marston Fitch (1909–2000) to undermine the obsession of 1970s U.S. preservation with the colonial period. He attacked the darling preservation project of the establishment: Colonial Williamsburg was for him the worst kind of "archeological preservation." The entire town had been returned to 1776 through surgical demolitions and scientific reconstructions, then furnished and perpetually maintained in first-class condition. The archaeological operations to "purify and telescope historic processes" presented visitors with a "simultaneity of well-being that would seldom if ever have occurred."[1] The experience distanced life from the past instead of bringing it closer.

Fitch's attacks on Colonial Williamsburg undermined the authority of the conventional preservation aesthetic of total restoration, which had reigned supreme in America since the 1920s. He diverted that authority to his own advantage, imposing his own variant of preservation poetics as the only legitimate one. He achieved this heretical reversal by gathering to himself the power generated by the social functioning of preservation's *illusio,* which he did not dare disturb.

Fitch proclaimed that historic preservation poetics had entered a new era in the late 1960s. Behind were the days when the total restoration of the object's material integrity was thought to be the royal road to returning life to the past. Total restoration had become a problem rather than a solution, because it transposed preservation poetics into invariance, effectively negating its character as the aesthetic expression of a temporal process. The practice of total restoration seemed elitist to Fitch: only the preservationist actually performing the restoration could experience preservation as a creative poetic process. The rest of society was reduced to passive spectatorship of the final aesthetic product. In addition, total restoration seemed to replicate high modern architecture's notion of design as a process restricted to professionals. This seemed anachronistic at a time when postmodern architects were

Future Anterior
Volume IV, Number 2
Winter 2007

2. Columbia University historic preservation students Brigitte Cook, Jill Hall, and Lewis Gleason measuring Venturi and Rauch's reconstruction of Benjamin Franklin's home. Photograph by author, 2003.

critiquing the lonely figure of the architect-hero, and experimenting with more inclusive processes of "community design." It was time, thought Fitch, to democratize preservation and to engage visitors in the process of making preservation, in its poetics. What Fitch meant by democratizing preservation poetics was something far more subtle than simply handing over design decisions to the public. The new preservation poetic involved striving toward an aesthetic that indexed its own making.

Venturi and Rauch's 1976–78 reconstruction of Benjamin Franklin's 1780s home in Philadelphia was, for Fitch, the emblematic example of this new preservation poetic: "a new level of maturity in American preservation."[2] The U.S. National Park Service originally planned to reconstruct Franklin's home as a traditional house museum complex. The market street rental houses were in fact reconstructed in the "typical" architectural language of the 1780s. Behind this new street wall, they also planned to reconstruct Franklin's print shop and house, but historians were unable to find sufficient historical documentation to determine the exact aesthetics of the original house. Venturi and Rauch proposed to acknowledge the limits of historical knowledge by proposing to reconstruct only those facts about the house and print shop that were archeologically and historically verifiable and letting visitors imagine the rest. They built a white steel frame that outlined the volume of the two structures as dematerialized "ghosts."[3] On the ground, the diagram of the floor plan was "drawn" on the pavement with walls indicated in white marble against a dark field of bluestone. In the absence of the usual material artifacts that would have cued visitors about whether they were standing in a kitchen or a bedroom, the three-dimensional diagram was "labeled" with inscriptions on the bluestone slabs: "You are now in the first floor area which served as a book bindery." Other didactic aesthetic devices also served to organize the visitor's attention toward archaeologically verifiable material "evidence" of history. Concrete "periscopes" punctured through the plane of pavers to reveal the archeological remains of the cellar below the house. Fitch praised Venturi and Rauch for combining the "cognitive and the sensuously perceptible" and turning the architecture itself into a "brilliant interpretation of the morphological development of the site," which was more engaging than a simple reconstruction.[4]

This was indeed a significant shift in preservation poetics. Since its neoclassical origins, the preservation practice of total reconstruction constituted historical meaning through the material expression of synthetic unity. To reconstitute the material unity of old architecture was really to return subjective intention to it through the medium of the contemporary architect, whose own intentionality came to stand in for the unrecoverable original. The contemporary architect's intention was brought under the compulsion of the historic artifact and guided toward the past through the struggle of preservation poetics. The architect's ethical choice to submit his creativity to the logic of the historic building did not diminish his authority as the legislating subject charged with bringing contemporary meaning back to history.

Venturi and Rauch's attack on the taboo of integrity recast preservation poetics as the process of disintegrating the architectural object. Poetically, this represented the sacrifice of the contemporary preservationist as the legislating subject. At first glance, this would appear as the triumph of scientific archeological "objectivity" and the liquidation of poetics altogether. But this would be too simplistic. The sacrifice of the legislating subject was also a refusal of subjective intention to be ruled by the "dead" architectural language of the past. To reconstruct the Franklin House in the manner of the 1780s would be to employ an architectural language so general that it would reduce what was to be expressed to something already given and known. Venturi and Rauch rose up in protest against the tyranny of "objective" restoration and tried to incorporate the subject and its expression into the language of objectivity. What made their intervention a new preservation poetic was the measure of their response. They did not try to counteract the violence that the scientific requirement for "objective"

3. 1970s reconstruction of the Market Street Rental Houses at the site of Benjamin Franklin's home. Photograph by author, 2003.

synthesis performed on the subject with the equivalent violence of a legislating subject who would dictate a totally contemporary aesthetic for the intervention à la Scarpa. Instead, they reintroduced subjectivity to preservation poetics as an aesthetic synthesis that knows itself to be inconclusive.

Without aesthetic unity there would be no hope that the material remains of the past could ever be meaningful to the living; there would be nothing in architecture but an inherently chaotic nature in diffuse form. This work of Venturi and Rauch bears witness to the 1970s moment when preservation diverged decisively from archaeology. Whereas archeology negated contemporary subjectivity within historical aesthetics, preservation, by detaching its poetics from empirical reality, created an aesthetic that lamented the sacrifice of subjectivity. Fitch helped prepare the theoretical ground from which this new preservation aesthetic sprung. Four decades before Venturi and Rauch's project, he had already recognized that preservation would only find adequate aesthetic expression under conditions of anonymity.[5] Seventy years on, we are only beginning to realize the radical position that preservation occupies within the field of aesthetic practices.

Endnotes

[1] James Marston Fitch, *Historic Preservation: Curatorial Management of the Built World* (Charlottesville: University Press of Virginia, 1990), 99.

[2] Ibid., 303. Venturi and Rauch collaborated with architect John Miller and with the exhibit design firm of de Martin-Marona and Associates on the preservation of Benjamin Franklin's house.

[3] Since the whole site above ground was "dematerialized," the spaces for traditional exhibits and film projections were buried out of sight.

[4] Fitch, *Historic Preservation,* 304.

[5] James Marston Fitch, "The Houses We Live In: An Anonymous Lament," in *Selected Writings on Architecture, Preservation, and the Built Environment,* ed. Martica Sawin, 26–40 (New York: W.W. Norton, 2006); originally published in *Architecture* 68 (October 1933): 213–18.

In This Issue

Le Corbusier, Giedion, and the Villa Savoye:
From Consecration to Preservation of Architecture
Panayotis Tournikiotis
Panayotis Tournikiotis describes the cooperation of Siegfried
Giedion and Le Corbusier that began at the first CIAM in 1928
and continued in 1930 with the publication of Giedion's article
in the *Cahiers d'Art,* written as the Villa Savoye was under
construction, which linked the new architecture directly to
Le Corbusier and the Villa. The cooperation reached its culmination in 1959 with an integrated communications campaign to save the villa. Giedion and Le Corbusier attempted
to find sponsors to purchase and renovate the house and a
new cultural use that would indirectly ensure protection in
the fullness of time; but it did not cross their minds that the
Villa should be designated a historic monument. However,
Corbusier's disciples and French Cultural Minister André
Malraux projected a different outcome: the Villa became the
first designated monument of modernism and the first case
for preserving modern architecture in the terms we understand today.

(Un)making Idolatry: From Mecca to Bamiyan
Jamal J. Elias
Jamal J. Elias describes the 2001 destruction of the Bamiyan
Buddhas in Afganistan at the hands of the ruling Taliban militia. Elias argues that Western accounts of the Taliban's actions
have failed to take into account the unfolding of events in the
context of the Islamic calendar and religious holidays and,
moreover, failed to survey the range of opinions in the Urdu-
language Pakistani press, the media with the most direct ties
to the Taliban leadership. Elias also argues that varying Muslim traditions of anti-idolatry were not the deciding factor in
the Taliban's decision to eliminate the Buddhas. Instead,
Elias argues that the confluence of heightened Muslim historical memory during the religious holidays, in conjunction with

Western pleas to save them, converted the Buddhas into idols that the Taliban felt they had no choice but to destroy.

Takings
Catherine Ingraham

Catherine Ingraham's "Takings" concerns the influences of Giorgio Agamben's term "bio-juridical"—which is, in truth, an equation—on historic preservation and architecture. The article discusses the relation of property (things) to rights (people). The Tugendhat House in Brno, Czech Republic, is used as an example of how property that is "taken" and then "kept" preserved as a historic artifact produces a clash of genealogical and teleological claims. These include the usual claims—such as those of family versus state, house versus architectural icon—as well as unusual claims such as those exerted by "taken" and "kept" objects.

Leopoldo Torres Balbás: Architectural Restoration and the Idea of "Tradition" in Early Twentieth-Century Spain
Juan Calatrava

Juan Calatrava examines the career of Leopoldo Torres Balbás (1888–1960), the preeminent theorist of historic preservation in twentieth-century Spain, who also served as an important architect, conservator, and architectural and urban historian. Calatrava places Torres Balbás within the "Generación del '98," artists and intellectuals who sought to define the essence of "Spanishness" in culture and in architecture in particular. In this debate, Calatrava argues, Torres Balbás provided the critical voice in championing the revalorization of the idea of tradition and the integration of popular architecture with modernity. Calatrava argues that, despite his marginalization under the Franco regime and his removal from directorship of the Alhambra, Torres Balbás's ideas and impressive scholarship remained the underpinning of both Spanish preservation and architectural theories well into the postwar period.

The Postmodern Cult of Monuments
Mario Carpo

Mario Carpo argues that the contemporary cult of brick-and-mortar monuments is predicated on surviving, or revived, cultural and technical premises, mostly inherited from the nineteenth century, that today may be partially flawed, obsolete, and ineffective at best. Today's memorial programs and functions are increasingly challenged by changes that have occurred in the contemporary philosophy of history: historical monuments may have a reduced significance in post-historical times. At the same time, digital information technologies are removing deeply rooted memorial traditions from physical space: the combined effects of electronic transference and of digital replication may foster the rise of new memorial practices to the detriment of old ones. This pattern suggests that monuments in stone may be destined to play a lesser role in the future than they have in the past. In this context, it is not surprising that the Postmodernist renaissance of monuments that we have been witnessing for the last twenty years (or longer) should inspire uneasiness, discomfort, or even alarm.

Architecture from Architecture:
Encounters between Conservation and Restoration
Manuel J. Martín-Hernández

Manuel J. Martín-Hernández argues that new developments in conservation theory, as reflected in the Krakow Charter (2000), have important implications for how we understand architectural interventions in historic environments. The new stress on the relationship between conservation and restoration suggests that architects might conceptualize their contemporary interventions as the development of the historic architecture through its continuous "re-design." But for this to occur, he argues, it is important that architects acquire the knowledge and ability to see in the historic building itself the lines of its future development.

Preservation through Contemporary Art
and Architecture

The Thyssen-Bornemisza Art Contemporary (T-B A21), under the leadership of Francesca von Habsburg, convened experts from the worlds of preservation, art, and architecture to a series of intimate roundtables, which took place in the island of Lopud, Croatia between June 18 and 20, 2007, as part of the symposium "Patronage of Space." The roundtable "Preservation through Contemporary Art and Architecture," transcribed in this issue, considered the relationship between two major works, one of preservation and the other of art and architecture, recently commissioned by T-B A21 on the island: the restoration of the Franciscan monastery, fortress, and Renaissance gardens that make up Lopud's monumental ensemble; and the Your Black Horizon pavilion by artist Olafur Eliasson and architect David Adjaye. The participants explored the capacity of contemporary interventions in historic environments to spur sustainable cultural, social, economic, and environmental development. The discussion also considered these interventions as stimulating opportunities to expand the operative range of contemporary art, architecture, and preservation.

1. Le Corbusier and Giedion at the fancy-dress ball that followed the signing of the Declaration at the First International Congress of Modern Architecture (CIAM), on June 28, 1928 (FLC L4-14-60). Photograph copyright Fondation Le Corbusier, Paris.

Panayotis Tournikiotis

Le Corbusier, Giedion, and the Villa Savoye
From Consecration to Preservation of Architecture

In its final verdict, on December 22, 1927, the League of Nations rejected the modern building that Le Corbusier and Pierre Jeanneret had proposed for its headquarters next to Lake Geneva, choosing instead a palace that featured conservative architecture of an academic character. This verdict was the starting point for an explosive campaign by Le Corbusier for the formulation of programmatic principles and strategies to ensure that modern architecture would prevail internationally. The campaign was very successful in Switzerland, which recognized in his person a child of its own. In this militant environment, Le Corbusier was the principal lever in the formation of the International Congresses of Modern Architecture (CIAM), which was achieved on June 28, 1928, at the Château de La Sarraz in Switzerland, near Lausanne, by the signing of the Declaration. Another Swiss from Zurich, Sigfried Giedion, proved to be an ally of Le Corbusier from the very beginning. Giedion had published a book on construction in iron and ferroconcrete in France that had included the works of Le Corbusier.[1] Together they wrote the *Working Programme* of the Congress and formulated the text of the Declaration, which was published by Giedion in German. Le Corbusier was the mastermind of the founding Congress and Giedion the secretary.[2] At the meetings it became apparent that there was no unanimity among the delegates, who were divided into different factions, but the common constituent of the views of Le Corbusier and Giedion was obvious and found expression in the dominance of the logic of construction as distilled into the five points of the new architecture—pilotis, free plan, free façade, flat roof, and ribbon windows, all of which were allowed by the functional independence of skeleton and wall. By this time, the channels of communication between Giedion and Le Corbusier were numerous and open.

On his return to Paris, Le Corbusier undertook, in September 1928, the design of the Villa Savoye, in which he tried to realize programmatically the basic principles of modern architecture that he had recently upheld, in dialogue with Giedion, at the La Sarraz Congress. Construction began in April 1929 and was virtually completed within a year, but much still remained to be done before the house was finally habitable in 1931. At the same period, Christian Zervos attempted to enlarge the

Future Anterior
Volume IV, Number 2
Winter 2007

1

circle of interest of the *Cahiers d'Art* in the direction of modern architecture and entrusted the editing of the relevant pages to Giedion. During the course of their collaboration, Giedion authored numerous articles and promoted architecture from the international modern scene, together with other subjects such as cinema and photography.[3]

In the fourth issue of 1930, Giedion wrote his most interesting article, "Le Corbusier and Contemporary Architecture."[4] The article was illustrated with twenty-one pictures of the Villa Savoye, and its last four pages were dedicated exclusively to the Villa, after the intervening title of "La Maison Savoye à Poissy, 1928–1930." In three successive moves, Giedion recognized in the "new architecture . . . a movement that can *today* be defined with precision,"[5] attributed to Le Corbusier the leading role in shaping the ideas and works of this movement, and pointed to the Villa Savoye as an exemplary building of the new architecture. The definitive factor in the progress of this architecture was not the evolution of its forms but the manner of construction, which was highlighted in a frame of supporting pillars and which permitted horizontal windows, gave flexibility to the façade and the ground plan, transformed the roof into a terrace, and left the ground floor space free: in other words, it was a built transcription of the five points of the new architecture.

This founding schema linking the new architecture to Le Corbusier and the Villa Savoye was written as the villa was under construction. Giedion visited the site at regular intervals and began the second part of his article by writing:

> We publish Le Corbusier's Savoye residence, which has just been completed. We have followed its construction at intervals of a few months until it took its present form, and we have tried to depict by means of photographs some of the views of the house as we saw it.[6]

In a series of letters exchanged between Giedion and Zervos from February through June 1930, there is a record of Giedion's difficult labor pains to photograph the unfinished building in a way that would make it appear finished. This exchange culminated in a letter from Zervos to Giedion dated June 4, 1930:

> Jeanneret has taken 30 photographs of the Savoye residence. His photographer told me that they are good. I shall have them this evening. In this way I shall supplement the photographs and I shall choose the best. Tomorrow we will send you the films and a print of the photographs that you took with me. . . . I have given the new copy of the text to be translated.[7]

LE CORBUSIER
ET L'ARCHITECTURE CONTEMPORAINE

par S. GIEDION

FONDATION LE CORBUSIER

And on June 10, 1930, Zervos wrote to Giedion again: "I trust that your love of photography will not be offended if I tell you that we have kept very few of the photographs which you took, since those of the photographer are based on your experience."[8]

The result is impressive. Giedion's photographs show us a house in various stages of construction, with the presence of the human figure providing the scale.[9] In one of these, Le Corbusier and Pierre Jeanneret are walking, deep in thought, on the formwork of the sitting room ceiling.[10] In a number of photographs, the planting of the "hanging garden" is well advanced, but the house is not yet habitable.[11] It would be no exaggeration to say that Giedion followed closely the gestation of the Villa Savoye and recorded every moment of its slow birth, thus giving by means of photographs and text a symbolic dimension to a work that was in creation, before it had been completed. The consecration of this residence as a supreme work of the new architecture was thus proposed in the process of its construction and was confirmed symbolically four years later. In 1934, Giedion wrote the introduction to the second volume of Le Corbusier's *Oeuvre complète 1929–1934,* which opens with nine richly illustrated pages on the

Villa Savoye.[12] In his introduction, Giedion argues that "Le Corbusier is at the very center of contemporary architecture" and goes on to an account of the five points of the new architecture, of which "the Villa Savoie *[sic]* is the purest and clearest example."[13] The circle closed with *Space, Time and Architecture,* in which Giedion gave an account of the five points of the new architecture and the Villa Savoye, with reference to his article of 1930 and the repetition of a number of its paragraphs.[14]

The *script*—the words and the photographs together—constituted the real construction of the Villa Savoye as an architectural symbol of the modern movement, and Giedion took part in this process as a real godfather. It is, then, in no way curious that thirty years later, when Le Corbusier learned that his "consecrated" work was threatened, he immediately turned to Giedion for support, who was then a professor at Harvard University.

The facts are well known.[15] The Savoyes lived in the villa until World War II; it was then commandeered by the Germans and subsequently passed to the Americans. When it returned to the Savoyes, they were no longer in a position to live as they had done before the war. Poissy had changed strikingly, the estate was large, and the house was abandoned. The municipality expropriated the Savoye property in order to put up school buildings. Le Corbusier was informed by the family on February 24, 1959, and immediately took action in every direction. The following day, he sent a telegram and wrote a letter to Giedion—who was at sea, on his way from Paris to New York—to report the situation and seek his help.[16]

Le Corbusier had specific aims that he desired from Giedion. The first of the desiderata was an intervention in the expropriation of the estate and the villa by the Municipality of Poissy.[17] However, the cancellation of this procedure was out of the question; instead, what was at issue was saving the villa, to be achieved by its purchase. Le Corbusier informed Giedion of actions already taken over the matter: the interest in saving the villa shown, regardless of his own wishes, by the Circle of Architectural Studies of Paris; his personal contacts with André Malraux, Minister for Cultural Affairs, "which took place in the best of conditions"; and the contact with UNESCO, which had been briefed on the matter by the mediation of a third party but did not have the money for the purchase. Le Corbusier had conveyed to UNESCO, however, that "Giedion is in touch with an American foundation (?) in order to secure the necessary sum and to determine the use of the villa and its park." There is absolutely no indication of the slightest intention of having the Villa Savoye listed as a historic monument. The objective was, rather, that the money should be located for a new owner to buy the villa and to determine its new use at a later date. To that end, Le Corbusier expected much of Giedion: that he should find money from American institutions, that he should make proposals on the villa's future use, and that he should mount a communications campaign to prompt the interest of the public in the architectural value of the villa and the need to preserve it. He stressed to Giedion at the end of the letter that "if there is a serious proposal from America in collaboration with UNESCO in Paris, an intervention by Malraux could probably be ensured," and he added: "this is, my dear Giedion, the program. Give the details of your proposal at once (financial data, administration, intentions, aim of the foundation, etc., etc.)."

It is clear that Le Corbusier did not expect much from the French, that he put a large part of his hopes in American money and institutions with cultural aims that were as yet undefined, and that he had a directness of communication with Giedion, on whom he believed he could rely. And he was right, to judge from the correspondence that followed. Giedion replied to him on March 5, 1959, from Harvard.[18] He had mobilized everyone, he had written to Roth, he had spoken to the Museum of Modern Art to get them to telegraph Malraux, and he had ensured the publication of an article in *Time* titled "The Story of the Savoye House." But the problem was, Giedion wrote, "the money is not deposited in the bank. Much more effort and work is needed for us to find it, but . . . I believe it is possible." In order for this money to be found, he asked Le Corbusier to immediately clarify three things for him: "1°/ *The price which Poissy paid for the expropriation.* The Americans do not pay out in a vacuum! We must know this in order to prevent the disaster and to be able to ask for the SUM. 2°/ *Your own* estimate of the cost of *renovation.* 3°/ For what purpose would you want to use the house and the sums you have already secured."[19] Giedion proved himself as able a manager as he was a historian. He did not lose himself in sentimental details, he did not use superfluous and empty words, and he did not extol (again) the value of the Villa Savoye; rather he spoke directly and in command like a general with a mission. He ended the letter in the same spirit: "From the American point of view it is impossible to ask for money without knowing the exact sum and the use to which it will be put." Giedion promised to mediate with the ideal American of whom Le Corbusier had dreamt since the 1930s. Significantly, Giedion did not raise question of the preservation of a historic monument.

Le Corbusier added his own comments to Giedion's handwritten letter and a few actions he thought of taking. Then he replied to Giedion on March 11, 1959, clearing up two of the

③ mais, c'est encore loin .

à quel but vous voudriez avoir utilisé la maison et les sommes nécessaires pour ce but.

J'étais déjà en contact avec le museum of modern Art, qui a, je crois, câblé aussi à Malraux et qui viendra, comme j'ai entendu de Jean Burckhardt en avril à Washington.

J'avais la visite du représentant du TIME-MAGAZIN, qui publiera probablement the Story of the Savoie House. I did what I could auf Seyt too. mais il faut savoir l'argent qu'il faut. Il est du point de vue américain impossible de demander des sommes sans savoir combien et exactement sous quelles circonstance.

Amicalement

[signature: Giedion]

que le ... commission d'arbitrage ... se réalise ...

3. The first page of the letter sent by Giedion to Le Corbusier on March 5, 1959 (FLC H1-12-187). Copyright Fondation Le Corbusier, Paris.

three issues with precision: "One hundred millions. Install Lecorbusier Foundation." These six words were repeated in the letter, as (?) he unpacked his reasoning.[20] The calculation of the necessary sum was based on the estimates of the specialist agronomists as to the estate and its fruit trees, which amounted to 105 and 25 million francs, respectively, with Le Corbusier considering that "a hundred million is a good compromise." The important thing, however, was the use. The following is the complete passage:

6

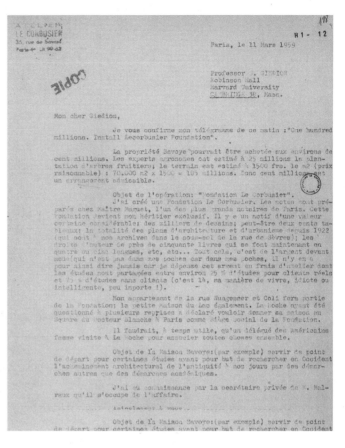

Object of the operation: "Fondation Le Corbusier."

I have set up a Le Corbusier Foundation. Its articles have been prepared by Maître Maguet, one of Paris's greatest notaries. This Foundation becomes my sole heir. There is an asset of very significant value: thousands of drawings; some two hundred paintings; the whole of the architectural and urban planning designs from 1922 onward (which are in our archives in the basement in the rue de Sèvres); the royalties on about fifty books which are available now in four or five languages, etc., etc.... All this money which is in front of us (*[sic]* it is never in my pockets because my pockets never had it, since I spent it on the expenses of the atelier, the designs of which were divided into approximately 25% of designs for actual clients and 75% of designs without clients (this is a way of life, idiotic or smart, it matters little!).

My apartment in Nungesser et Coli Street will be part of the Foundation; the little House on the Lake as well. La Roche, who has been asked many times, has said that he wants to give his house in the Square du Docteur Blanche in Paris as the official Headquarters of the Foundation.

A representative of the Americans should in due course visit La Roche in order to tie all these things together.

The aim of the Savoye House: (for example) to be a base for some studies which will have the purpose of investigating in the West the course of architecture from antiquity to our own time by methods different from academic methods.

This is in effect the whole of the letter, though Le Corbusier significantly mentioned in a final sentence that he also "met M. Malraux's personal assistant who is dealing with the affair."

The American money was not found, nor did it need to be found. The villa remained in the ownership of the municipality. The Le Corbusier Foundation was set up, and everything that Le Corbusier had outlined happened, except for the directive on the Villa Savoye. In that direction the French energy was decisive, with the personal intervention of André Malraux, to whose desk, it seems, telegrams and letters arrived from all over the world, thanks to Giedion, who played a major role. We can read their impact and the intelligent mise en scène of the whole protest in a letter that Le Corbusier addressed exactly a year later, on March 11, 1960, to Pierre Sonrel, president of the Circle of Architectural Studies of Paris, who, although he had played a part in the rescue operation from the very beginning, clearly had other aims.[21] Le Corbusier attacked him to secure his own participation in the decisions on the use and status to be accorded to the Villa Savoye and at the same time defended himself over the major operation he had orchestrated:

> The Savoye affair broke out totally and completely unknown to me by the agency of a foreign architect who was passing through Paris, and hearing talk about the demolition of the Villa Savoye, informed Giedion at Harvard, who was able and knew how to act, from where he was, in a particularly brilliant way, because within a few days M. Malraux received on his desk 250 telegrams from all over the world. I was in India. I learned of all this when I returned. There was an important meeting at the Ministry of M. Malraux on the status to be accorded to the Villa Savoye, on the status of the estate and its probable intended use. Decisions were made. I also made proposals on the use of the Villa Savoye."[22]

But the die had been cast on March 9, 1959, when Giedion wrote from Harvard, for reasons that had been predetermined in the cultural policy of Malraux without having yet been recorded. André Malraux, famous *homme des lettres,* was State minister in January 1959 and had launched the first French Ministry of Cultural Affairs in February 1959 as well as proclaimed a new policy for the preservation of cultural heritage, including architecture. Hence the Villa Savoye easily received the "protection d'un véritable monument historique," as requested by Alfred Roth, an old working fellow and disciple of Le Corbusier and, in 1959, dean of the Zurich School of Architecture, in a letter to the French minister, also on March 9, 1959, written at the prompting of Giedion.[23] The reaction was lightning and the timing perfect. However, through this, the paradigmatic building of the new architecture that in 1930 was establishing Giedion's new tradition and the ambitious headquarters for research into the history of architecture by nonacademic methods that Le Corbusier envisioned thirty years later was strikingly recognized as a *historic monument.* The Villa Savoye would be the first building of modern architecture listed as historic in France[24] and the first building to be the object of a preservation order while its architect was still living, partly as a result of the architect's own initiative.[25] The Ministry of Cultural Affairs made Jean Dubuisson, architect of the École des Beaux Arts, Premier Grand Prix de Rome, and Architecte en chef des bâtiments civils et palais nationaux — precisely titles and institutions that Le Corbusier curtly rejected throughout the 1920s and 1930s — responsible for the restoration of the Villa Savoye. Nevertheless, Le Corbusier worked with him, and on June 3, 1965, Dubuisson submitted to him the plans and the report on the design for the full restoration of the historic monument. Le Corbusier studied it carefully, added to it, confirmed it, and disagreed with it on twenty-six typewritten pages on July 6, 1965, less than two months before his death on August 27, 1965. But the villa was "re-baptized," now unchanged by the decay of time, its sole use the image of itself. Consecration and preservation at one and the same time.

The meeting and collaboration of Le Corbusier and Giedion, which began in 1928 and continued in 1930 with the paradigmatic publication of the Villa Savoye, reached its culmination in 1959 with the integrated communications operation for its rescue, even if that rescue was not in the terms they had in mind. They attempted to find sponsors and a new cultural use that would be in keeping with the architectural shell and would indirectly ensure protection in the fullness of time, but it did not cross their minds that the villa should become a historic monument. This was sought by the disciples; it was demanded by the moment in history, it was Malraux's wish, and the first case for preserving modern architecture in the terms we understand nowadays. In the case of the Villa Savoye, the book in the end *did not kill the building,* as Victor Hugo, with a view to preserving the past, warned one hundred and twenty years earlier in *Notre-Dame de Paris.* The book *became* the eternal building. For Giedion and Le Corbusier, and

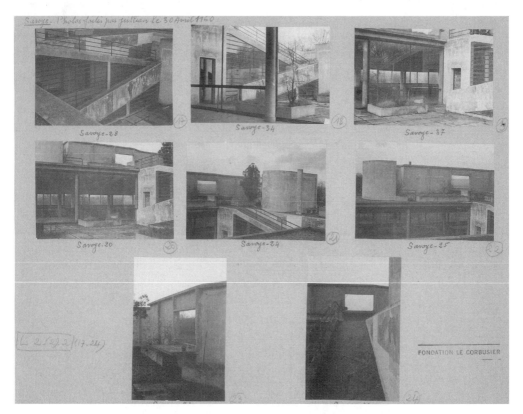

FONDATION LE CORBUSIER

5. The Villa Savoye as photographed by Jullian on April 30, 1960, before any preservation work (FLC L2-17-136). A comparison of these photographs with those of the *Cahiers d'Art* of 1930 reveals a remarkable resemblance. Photograph copyright Fondation Le Corbusier, Paris.

for the history of modern architecture, the *script*—the words and the photographs together—was the definitive construction of the architecture.

Author Biography
Panayotis Tournikiotis is associate professor of architectural theory at the National Technical University of Athens, School of Architecture, and chair of the DoCoMoMo International Specialist Committee on Register. He studied architecture, town planning, and philosophy. He is author of *Adolf Loos* (1991), *The Historiography of Modern Architecture* (1999), and *Architecture in Our Time* (2006). He is also editor of *The Parthenon and Its Impact in Modern Times* (1994), and the Greek translator of Le Corbusier's *Vers une architecture* (2004). His current work is concerned with Le Corbusier in the 1920s and 1930s.

Endnotes
Translated by Geoffrey Cox. I would like to thank the Fondation Le Corbusier in Paris for its ready support of my research in 2005 and 2007—particularly its director, Michel Richard, and its archivist, Arnaud Dercelles. My thanks also go to the John F. Costopoulos Foundation, in Athens, for its kind support of my studies of the work of Le Corbusier.
[1] Sigfried Giedion, *Bauen in Frankreich, Bauen in Eisen, Bauen in Eisenbeton* (Leipzig: Klinkhardt & Biermann, 1928); *Building in France, Building in Iron, Building in Ferroconcrete*, trans. J. Duncan Berry (Santa Monica, Calif.: Getty Research Institute for the History of Arts and the Humanities, 1995).
[2] On the first CIAM, see Jacques Gubler, *Nationalisme et internationalisme dans l' architecture moderne de la Suisse*, 2nd ed. (Geneva: Archigraphie, 1988), 145–61, and Martin Steinmann, *CIAM Dokumente 1928–1939, Internationale Kongresse für Neues Bauen* (Basel: Birkhauser, 1979).
[3] Christian Derouet, "Siegfried Giedion: la page d' architecture des Cahiers d'Art, 1928–1934," *Les Cahiers du MNAM* 82 (Winter 2002–2003): 42–65.
[4] S. Giedion, "Le Corbusier et l' architecture contemporaine," *Cahiers d'Art* 4 (1930): 204–15.
[5] Ibid., 205. The emphasis is mine.
[6] Ibid., 212.

[7] Derouet, "Siegfried Giedion," 55. Giedion's correspondence with Zervos is kept in the archives of the GTA in Zurich. The photographs that Giedion took during this collaboration have been deposited in the Kandinsky Library of the Centre Pompidou in Paris.

[8] Ibid.

[9] Giedion, "Le Corbusier et l' architecture contemporaine," 207.

[10] Ibid., 211.

[11] Ibid., 213–15.

[12] S. Giedion, "Préface aux œuvres de Le Corbusier 1929–1934," in *Le Corbusier et Pierre Jeanneret, œuvre Complète de 1929–1934*, ed. Willy Boesiger, 7–9 (Zurich: Girsberger, 1935). The Villa Savoye is described in pages 23–31, after Le Corbusier's introduction. The only features in the rich illustration of the Villa Savoye that it has in common with the description in *Cahiers d'Art* are the three floor plans.

[13] Ibid., 7.

[14] Sigfried Giedion, *Space, Time, and Architecture* (Cambridge, Mass.: Harvard University Press, 1941; 5th edition, 1965), 524–30.

[15] See Kevin D. Murray, "The Villa Savoye and the Modernist Historic Monument," *Journal of the Society of Architectural Historians* 61, no. 1 (March 2002): 68–89, and Jacques Sbriglio, *Le Corbusier: La Villa Savoye / The Villa Savoye* (Basel: Birkhäuser, 1999), 150–68.

[16] FLC H1-12-182.

[17] The compulsory purchase appeared to be a faît accompli, but the arbitration committee that fixed the sum of the compensation met on April 28, 1960, and payment was made on December 30, 1960 (FLC U1-15-214). The sum paid amounted to 90,000,000 francs (approximately 1,300,000 € at 2005 prices).

[18] FLC H1-12-187.

[19] The underlining and capitals are in the original (see Figure 3).

[20] FLC H1-12-188.

[21] Pierre Sonrel had approached André Malraux—even before Le Corbusier had made a move—seeking to rescue the villa and accommodate the Circle of Architectural Studies of Paris there. On March 8, 1960, he reverted in writing to Malraux on precisely the same matter.

[22] FLC H1-12-299.

[23] FLC H1-12-191.

[24] It was the second building of the twentieth century listed, after the Theatre des Champs Elysées by Auguste Perret.

[25] The decree listing the Villa Savoye in the "bâtiments civils" is dated February 7, 1964, before Le Corbusier's death. The decree listing the Villa in the "monuments historiques" is dated December 16, 1965, four months after he died.

1. Afghan postal stamp showing the Bamiyan Buddhas.

Jamal J. Elias

(Un)making Idolatry
From Mecca to Bamiyan

> I ask the Afghans and the Muslims of the world: Would
> you rather be the smashers of idols or the sellers of idols?
>> Mullah Umar, supreme leader of Taliban

> It is not those who forget, but those who "remember"
> the past that are condemned to repeat it.
>> Sheldon Pollock, "Ramayana and Political
>> Imagination in India"

On February 26, 2001, Mullah Umar, the Supreme Leader of
the Taliban militia ruling most of Afghanistan, ordered the
destruction of all statues in areas under Taliban control. Starting on March 2, the Taliban embarked on an extended campaign using dynamite, anti-aircraft guns, and other heavy
weapons to destroy the two best-known pre-Islamic relics in
the country, the Buddha statues of Bamiyan. Their construction began in the second century CE under the Buddhist king
Kanishka and was probably completed in the fifth century CE.
The taller, at 55 meters (175 feet), is believed to have been the
largest statue of the Buddha in the world; the smaller statue,
at 38 meters (115 feet) tall, also ranked among the largest surviving images of the Buddha. Through a thousand years of
Muslim rule they had suffered only sporadic, isolated attempts
at their destruction by particularly zealous iconoclasts. More
recently, they had been viewed as the centerpiece of Afghanistan's (albeit small) tourist industry and were promoted as a
symbol of the country's long heritage, appearing on postage
stamps and state-produced cultural publications before the
Soviet invasion of Afghanistan in 1979.

The obliteration of the Bamiyan Buddhas was accompanied by the destruction of most, if not all, of the Buddhist
figural art left in Taliban-controlled Afghanistan after two
decades of looting and bombing in the war against the Soviet
Union and the subsequent civil war. The six-week-long saga,
beginning on February 12, 2001, with the announcement of
the planned destruction of the Buddhas and ending shortly
after the confirmation of their destruction on March 26, unfolded amid a massive international campaign to save the
statues. Their destruction was widely condemned in the Western world, in countries with Buddhist and Hindu populations, as
well as in Islamic countries such as Afghanistan's neighbors

Future Anterior
Volume IV, Number 2
Winter 2007

Iran and Pakistan. Criticism of the Taliban by all parties, East and West, consisted of their vilification as intransigent philistines who were utterly intolerant of other religions and of the concepts of art, history, and world heritage.

This paper will attempt to contextualize the Taliban's actions by taking a close look at their statements and behavior as the events unfolded in February and March of 2001. It argues that the Taliban's destruction of the Buddhas was neither part of a preconceived plan based in an uncompromising and anachronistic view of Islam, nor was it a petulant political reaction to their rejection and isolation by the world community. On the contrary, throughout the weeks in question, the Taliban leadership was sensitive to both international and local public opinion; the discursive process surrounding their pronouncements concerning the Buddhas and others' reactions to them played a large part in shaping the Taliban's self-understanding.

Much has been written on Muslim attitudes toward idolatry. Finbarr Barry Flood has written an interesting article historicizing the Taliban's acts in an Islamic context in an attempt to show that their sort of iconoclasm is an aberration and not part of a universal Muslim attitude toward idols and images.[1] Islam shares with Judaism and Christianity a two-faceted distrust of visual and physical representation. On one side is the preference for the nonphysical over the physical, thought over matter, that pervades the philosophy of late antiquity and to which Islamic philosophical thinking is a direct heir. On the other is the scriptural prohibition against figural imagery. It is worth noting, nonetheless, that there is no clear Islamic condemnation paralleling the Biblical ban of the second commandment. Qur'anic condemnations are nowhere as explicit, perhaps the clearest being, "And Abraham said to his father Azar: Do you take idols *(asnāman)* as Gods? Indeed I see you and your people in a manifest error" (6:74). The ambivalence of Islamic attitudes toward idolatry and iconoclasm is evident in the following accounts of Muslim encounters with idols. Two are from the South Asian context and one from the formative period of Islam.

In September 1528, Babur, founder of the Mughal Empire in India, came to the town of Urwahi in Gwalior. His memoirs describe the incident as follows:

> Urwahi is surrounded on three sides by a single mountain, the stone of which is not so red as that of Bayana but somewhat paler. The solid rock outcroppings around Urwahi have been hewn into idols, large and small. On the southern side is a large idol, approximately twenty yards tall. They are shown stark naked with all their pri-

vate parts exposed. Around the two large reservoirs inside Urwahi have been dug twenty to twenty-five wells, from which water is drawn to irrigate the vegetation, flowers, and trees planted there. Urwahi is not a bad place. In fact, it is rather nice. Its one drawback was the idols, so I ordered them destroyed.[2]

The second example is from a description of the Indus valley (Al-Sind) by the renowned tenth-century Arab Muslim geographer al-Muqaddasi:

As for the idols in this region, there are two in Harawa made of stone: no one approaches them. They have a power such that should a man try to lay his hand on one, it will be held back and will not reach the idol. They both appear as though made of gold and silver. It is said that if one expresses a wish in their presence, the request will be granted.... The two statues are quite enchanting. I saw a Muslim man who said he had forsaken Islam to return to the worship of the idols, having been captivated by them; when he returned to Naysabur [in Iran] he became Muslim again. The two idols really are miraculous![3]

The final example is a popular account in a work by Ibn al-Kalbi, entitled *The Book of Idols,* of the destruction of al-'Uzza, a deity mentioned in the Qur'an. According to Ibn al-Kalbi, sometime around 630 C.E. Muhammad commanded his military champion Khalid ibn Walid to the valley of Nakhlah where there were three trees inhabited by the goddess al-'Uzza, and ordered him to cut down the first one. When Khalid reported back, Muhammad asked him if he had seen anything unusual there, to which Khalid ibn Walid replied that he had not. Khalid's return to cut down the second tree was similarly uneventful. When he returned to cut down the third tree, he encountered an Abyssinian woman with wild hair, gnashing and grating her teeth, accompanied by Dubayyah al-Sulami, the custodian of al-'Uzza. Dubayyah addressed the woman, calling her al-'Uzza and beseeching her to kill Khalid. The Muslim champion struck her with his sword, cutting off her head, at which she fell to the ground in a pile of ashes. He then killed her custodian, Dubayyah, felled the tree, and returned to Muhammad with his report. Muhammad allegedly commented: "That was al-'Uzza.... Verily she shall never be worshipped again."[4]

The implications of Ibn al-Kalbi's account of the killing of al-'Uzza are clear. Muhammad did not deny that al-'Uzza was *real.* She was not a mere tree that the ignorant pagan Arabs insisted on worshipping; Dubayyah, her custodian, did not try to stop Khalid ibn Walid himself but rather he beseeched the goddess to defend herself (and, by extension, those who worshipped her); and it took one of the greatest champions of Islam to kill al-'Uzza, a feat that presumably could only be accomplished because it was the will of the superior deity of Muhammad and Khalid ibn Walid.

Al-Muqqadisi's description of the Indian temple is similar in its open acknowledgment of the power of the idol. Clearly, neither he nor Ibn al-Kalbi denied the existence of supernatural power resident in idols; they simply saw them as doctrinally illegitimate and inferior both morally and in power to Islam and Allah. In contrast, Babur's iconoclastic act ostensibly was motivated not by religion as much as aesthetics: the vulgar statues of Urwahi were a stain on an otherwise very pleasant place.

These varied examples notwithstanding, Islam has an undeniable iconoclastic ethos similar to that of Judaism and most of Christianity. The Qur'an situates Muslim monotheism squarely within a Biblical prophet tradition in which Abraham is the protomonotheist who rejects the false gods of his ancestors. There are many instances of Muslims destroying Hindu idols for the express purpose of eliminating idolatry or marking the victory of Islam, and some Central and South Asian Muslim rulers proudly bore the title of "idol-destroyer" (but-shikan).

The Taliban's destruction of the Bamiyan Buddhas must be seen within the context of Muslim historical memory in which intolerance of idols can easily, if erroneously, be seen as woven into mores of proper Muslim behavior, and iconoclasm — if not always viewed as laudable — is never a popularly condemnable act.

Newspaper Coverage

The Taliban's destruction of the Buddhas in February and March of 2001 coincided with one of the holiest periods in the lunar Islamic year, called the Hijri calendar, which is used in most Muslim societies including Afghanistan. The Hajj pilgrimage, a central ritual that ends on Eid al-adha, the holiest day of the Muslim year, fell on March 3–6. The timeline leading up to the destruction of the Buddhas is therefore critical to understanding the Taliban's actions. I have provided the major dates in the Gregorian calendar with the corresponding Hijri date in parentheses:

1996 (1417): Taliban conquered Kabul for the first time, making them de facto rulers of Afghanistan.

1998 (1419): A preliminary attack was made on the smaller Buddha during the Taliban occupation of Bamiyan.

2. The Bamiyan Valley, Afghanistan, nineteenth-century view, looking northwest toward Buddha niches and monastic sanctuaries.

July 1999 (Rabi' al-awwal 1420): Supreme Leader of the Taliban, Mullah Umar, decreed protection for all non-Muslim relics, including the statues.

February 12, 2001 (19 Dhu'l-qa'da 1421): The BBC reported that Taliban representatives, invoking the Islamic prohibition against the depiction of living things, had destroyed over a dozen ancient statues in the Kabul National Museum.

February 26, 2001 (2 Dhu'l-hajjah 1421): Mullah Umar announced that all statues in the Taliban-controlled areas of Afghanistan were to be destroyed.[5] This was followed immediately by a statement issued through the Taliban Ambassador to Pakistan, Mullah Abdul Salam Zaeef: "Afghanistan's religious scholars and the Supreme Court have unanimously issued the *fatwa* which [will] be implemented at all costs." The decree is to be carried out jointly by the Ministries of Information and Culture and of Fostering Virtue and Preventing Vice.[6]

March 1, 2001 (5 Dhu'l-hajjah 1421): It was widely reported that the Taliban had started using heavy weapons to destroy the statues.

March 2, 2001 (6 Dhu'l-hajjah 1421): The Pakistan-based Afghan Islamic Press quoted Taliban sources as saying explosives were being brought to Bamiyan from other provinces and that all statues in Taliban-controlled areas were in the process of being demolished. India offered to take custody of the artifacts.[7]

March 5, 2001 (9 Dhu'l-hajjah 1421, the last day of the Hajj and eve of Eid al-adha): Mullah Umar defended his edicts, posing the rhetorical question: "I ask Afghans and the world's Muslims to use their sound wisdom. . . . do you prefer to be a smasher of idols or a seller of idols?"[8]

March 9, 2001 (13 Dhu'l-hajjah 1421, immediately after the Eid al-adha holiday): The Afghan Islamic Press (AIP) confirmed that demolition work had resumed after having been suspended for a few days.[9]

March 11, 2001 (15 Dhu'l-hajjah 1421): A joint UNESCO-OIC (Organization of the Islamic Conference) delegation arrived in Pakistan to plead with the Taliban, led by Qatar's Minister of State for Foreign Affairs, Zaid al-Mahmud, accompanied by Shaikh Nasr Farid Wassel, Mufti of Al-Azhar (the most prestigious religious institution in the Sunni world), as well as by another Al-Azhar-based scholar, Shaikh Muhammad al-Rawi; they were to be joined by Yusuf al-Qaradawi, the most popular preacher in the entire Arab world.

March 14, 2001 (18 Dhu'l-hajjah 1421): Taliban expelled BBC reporter Kate Clark and closed Kabul office of BBC, accusing her of biased reporting and calling the Taliban "ignorant."

March 16, 2001 (20 Dhu'l-hajjah 1421): The Afghan Foreign Minister, Wakil Ahmed Mutawakkil, announced that the destruction was not completed because snowfall caused a work stoppage. He simultaneously announced that the Taliban would continue to provide sanctuary to Osama bin Laden.[10]

March 19, 2001 (23 Dhu'l-hajjah 1421): Al-Jazeera showed footage of the destruction. The Taliban sacrificed one hundred cows to atone for the delay in destroying the statues.[11]

March 20, 2001 (24 Dhu'l-hajjah 1421): The U.S. government rejected Taliban claims that the statues' destruction was justified by an alleged UNESCO offer of money to save the statues when no money was offered for the starving people of Afghanistan. It also insisted that sanctions against Afghanistan would stand until bin Laden was handed over.

March 22, 2001 (26 Dhu'l-hajjah 1421): Journalists were taken on a tour of Afghanistan's national museum to see the results of the destruction there.

March 26, 2001 (1 Muharram 1422, New Year's Day in the Hijri calendar): Twenty journalists were flown to Bamiyan to see the destroyed statues.

November 11, 2001 (24 Sha'ban 1422): The Taliban destroyed the Bamiyan town they retreated in front of the advancing local militia, Hizb-e islami.

Western popular coverage of Taliban statements and actions was almost uniformly condemnatory through this period, with few journalists or analysts attempting to make sense of what the Taliban were doing. Statements by Mullah Umar saying the statues would be destroyed because they "have been used as idols and deities by the non-believers.... Only Allah, Most High, deserves to be worshipped, not anyone or anything else," and his infamous comment, "We do not understand why everybody is so worried.... All we are breaking are stones"[12] were quoted in the Western media primarily as examples of the Taliban's incomprehensible irrationality. Their actions were universally treated in the Western press as out of keeping with the will of the Afghan people, and the BBC went so far as to declare that the "majority" of Afghans inside the country were "devastated" by the destruction of the Buddhas.[13]

Coverage of the Taliban's actions after the fact in scholarly publications showed a similar tone. In one of several articles dealing with the Bamiyan Buddhas published in *iconoclash,* Jean-Michel Frodon stated, "It is against that community and against a relationship with the world that values a non-religious relationship with the invisible, that the dynamite which destroyed the giant Buddhas was used."[14] In another essay in the same collection, Jean-François Clément displayed no understanding of the nature of religious reformism when he mused about the implications the Taliban's behavior carried for their attitudes toward other Muslims and the future of Islam:

> By destroying the Buddhas, the Taliban were clearly signaling that all [Muslims] who had preceded them in Afghanistan, who had respected the statues, were not real [Muslims]. In short, there had never been [Muslims] before them. But will there be any after them? In the decree ordering the destruction of all representations of living creatures, the Taliban declared that the Bāmiyān Buddhas had to be destroyed because "Buddhism should return to Afghanistan." What strange [Muslims] were these who could foresee the impending disappearance of Islam.[15]

Significantly absent in the coverage of the events in Western-language publications is any indication that commentators had read the local press. The most remarkable aspect of this oversight is that, to the best of my knowledge, not one scholar or journalist who has written about the events bothered to look at the Islamic Hijri calendar used in Afghanistan, a major omission since the calendar played a central role in the proceedings. Mullah Umar's initial declaration ordering the destruction was made on 2 Dhu'l-hajja, five days before the start of the Hajj pilgrimage and eight days before Eid al-adha. The lead-up to the pilgrimage is a time of heightened religious sensitivity across the Muslim world, as pilgrims prepare for their departure for Mecca while the rest of the community participates vicariously in this major ritual. Eid al-adha itself commemorates Abraham's willingness to sacrifice his son and is popularly understood as a reminder to all Muslims to be ready to sacrifice all that is dear to them at God's command. Mullah Umar's choice of occasion can hardly be considered accidental, since the other major act for which Abraham is remembered is his decision to break from the idolatry of his father and ancestors, an obvious precedent on which the Taliban modeled their decision to right the wrongs of their forefathers in Afghanistan and destroy idols that they openly acknowledged were part of Afghanistan's pre-Islamic heritage. It is in this light that the animal sacrifice on March 19 (23 Dhu'l-hajja) makes most sense.[16]

The calendar was a central factor not just in evoking religious memory as the Taliban cast themselves as moral heirs to Abraham but also in the very progression of events. Demolition work was suspended for Eid al-adha, and there appears to have been a brief lull during which Mullah Umar was directly responsive to opinion from the Western and Islamic worlds. However, the high-level delegation of Muslim clerics was prevented from being assembled until March 11 (15 Dhu'l-hajja) by the same holiday. The Taliban's responses to statements and proposals from the West, which seemed oblivious to the symbolism of what the Taliban saw themselves as doing, were clearly colored by the calendar. Significant among these was the offer of New York City's Metropolitan Museum of Art, made through the United Nations, to pay for the removal of all moveable relics in Afghanistan. This offer came during the Hajj, at a time when the memory of Abraham could not be stronger, since both the Hajj and Eid al-adha commemorate events in Abraham's life, in particular his opposition to idols and his willingness to sacrifice his son for the sake of God. It is no wonder that such offers were widely reported in newspapers read by those sympathetic to the Taliban.

It is in the context of local opinion and media that the Taliban's actions come into clearest light. Given the almost complete absence of publishing in the Taliban's Afghanistan, their international isolation, strong ideological ties with religious groups in Pakistan, and the pattern of reliance on Pakistani resources forced on many Afghans through two decades of war, the local press to which the Taliban reacted most directly was that of Pakistan.

The emotional links between the Taliban and some religious elements in Pakistani society are very deep.[17] Most of the Taliban leadership was trained in Pakistani seminaries belonging to the Deobandi school of Sunni thought, a somewhat puritanical reform movement started in opposition to British colonial rule in India. Deobandi ideology, which teaches that a Muslim's primary loyalty is to the religion, not the nation-state, and actively encourages individuals to agitate for the political unification of the world's Muslim population, has a substantial and influential following in Pakistan. The majority of religious seminaries are run by Deobandis, and the political party associated with the school, the *Jamī'at-e 'ulamā-ye Islam* (henceforth JUI), has a disproportionate degree of influence in Pakistani politics. In many ways, the Taliban can be seen as the wayward children of the JUI, born in politicized seminaries and traumatized by the Afghan civil war. Large numbers of Pakistanis joined the Taliban and fought in Afghanistan in the late 1990s, and many more viewed the Taliban as ideologically admirable harbingers of a Muslim utopia. The Taliban, in turn, depended on Pakistan for education and military training, as well as economic and moral support. Though not always tractable in their decision making, there is no doubt that they were ever cognizant of the importance of Pakistani public opinion and shaped their policies to reflect that.

Very insightful work has been done concerning the difference between English and local-language media in India. In *Politics after Television,* Rajagopal demonstrates how the English-language media failed to see the growth of Hindu nationalism through the late 1980s and the 1990s. When the serialized *Ramayana* began in 1985, many found it significant only because it was the most-watched show in the country. The English-speaking self-proclaimed shapers and arbiters of public opinion were taken completely by surprise when this TV show became the fuel for the Ram Janam Bhoomi movement, which culminated in the destruction of the Babri Mosque on December 6, 1992.[18] The destruction of this mosque was widely condemned by the Pakistani public and its memory played a significant role in the Taliban's rhetoric.

In Pakistan, the relationship of language to newspapers is somewhat different, in the sense that Urdu, Pakistan's national language, is pervasively used. Not only can Urdu-language publications be considered mainstream, but Urdu newspapers of record also follow the same journalistic standards as English-language papers, unlike the other non-English press in India.

The English-language press in Pakistan echoed international opinion on the Taliban's behavior and was almost universally condemnatory. The *Pakistan Times,* one of the most widely read English papers, emphasized the following themes: (1) the need to preserve global heritage; (2) tolerance for other religions; (3) that Islam condemns destroying other people's places of worship; (4) in addition, that Islam mandates tolerance of other religions; (5) that these actions would make the world think Muslims were backward; and (6) that it would give justification to others to victimize Muslims and put Muslim historical sites and places of worship at risk. Through the period in question, only three letters in the *Pakistan Times* expressed ambivalence over the issue. They highlighted the hypocrisy of the international community's concern for dead stone in a country suffering a severe drought and a widening famine. None were supportive of the Taliban.[19]

In contrast, the Urdu press, read by the majority of Pakistan's population, published a much wider spectrum of opinion. The daily *Jang,* which is published by Pakistan's largest media group and employs a neutral reporting mode, provided extensive coverage of Taliban statements as well as reactions by Muslim clerics, some of whom supported the Taliban. It also displayed a much wider range of opinion in editorials and letters to the editor. The majority of letters to the editor in *Jang* brought up Western hypocrisy. Some specifically mentioned iconoclasm as a religious duty; complained of the lack of international concern when the Babri Mosque was destroyed a decade earlier, of an anti-Muslim bias in the West; and connected the sanctions on the drought-stricken people of Afghanistan to the persecution of Muslims in Bosnia, Chechnya, Kashmir, and the Palestinian Territories.

The Taliban's public statements should be seen in the context of Pakistan's Urdu press, where they seem the least irrational. Trying to justify the destruction of the statues, the Taliban and their sympathizers stressed four main points. In addition to the commonly made claim of the hypocrisy in concern over dead stone but not for living human beings, the Taliban and supporters argued that the statues were not objects of worship since there were no Buddhists in Afghanistan. As such, destroying them was not an act of desecration or persecution. Thus they pointed out that their actions were not out of line with Islamic injunctions to respect other religions, an accusation leveled against them from a number of quarters. Since no one worshipped the Buddhas, they were not covered by rules of protection that were extended to idols in Hindu

3. Nineteenth-century view of the taller Bamiyan Buddha, 55 meters (175 feet) tall, constructed second to fifth century CE.

temples and homes in Afghanistan. (In fact, the Taliban reacted very strongly to accusations that the destruction of the Buddhas was symptomatic of their treatment of religious minorities.) In direct contradiction to these points were statements made by Taliban spokesmen as well as sympathetic Pakistani clerics saying that the Taliban's acts were payback for the destruction of the Babri Mosque at the hands of Hindu militants.[20] Finally, the religious argument was linked to the accusation of hypocrisy on the part of the international community: the very fact that money was offered to save the statues transformed them from artifacts into idols since they were now being venerated more than human lives, and this reverence necessitated their destruction.

When Mullah Umar rhetorically asked the Afghan people and Muslims all over the world if they would rather be the smashers of idols or the sellers of them, he was clearly referring back to Sultan Mahmud of Ghazna, the Afghan iconoclast of myth and legend who sacked the Shiva temple at Somnath, Gujrat, in 1025 CE. The local priests and rulers

4. Nineteenth-century view of the
smaller Bamiyan Buddha.

allegedly offered a treasure to ransom the main Shiva Linga icon, and Mahmud is legendary for having replied that he was a smasher of idols, not a seller of them.[21] Mullah Umar was also referring to the prophet Abraham, who broke with the religion of his father Azar, a maker and seller of idols, and it was this latter claim that resonated in the popular press and was applauded by Taliban sympathizers. On March 2 (6 Dhu'l-hajja, the day before the Hajj starts), Abdul Akbar Chitrali, a provincial head of the *Jamī'at-e ittihād-e 'ulamā* (an organization supported by the JUI), declared that selling idols was wrong and congratulated the Taliban for reviving the "Tradition of Abraham" *(sunnat-e Ibrāhīmī)*.[22] The same sentiment was echoed at a high-level meeting of the JUI on the eve of Eid al-Adha, in which one prominent cleric, Hafiz Husayn Ahmad, made an explicit link between the timing of the Taliban's actions in the "month of sacrifice" and the tradition of Abraham. The head of the organization and then-leader of Pakistan's opposition, Maulana Fazlur Rahman, also applauded the Taliban and congratulated them for exposing Western hypocrisy.[23] The following week, other important members of the JUI gave wider legitimacy to the Taliban's actions by declaring that iconoclasm was the way of all prophets and that the Taliban had fulfilled "Prophetic Tradition" *(sunnat-e nabī),* an explicit reference to Muhammad.[24]

Even moderate religious voices were not necessarily condemnatory of the Taliban's actions. On the day commemorating Abraham's sacrifice, Maulana Shah Ahmad Nurani, leader of the *Jamī'at-e 'Ulamā-ye Pakistan,* the World Islamic Mission, and a man long recognized for his moderate views, said that destroying the Buddhas was the right thing to do.[25]

However, the overall tone of the most-respected Urdu paper was not supportive of the Taliban. The editorial on Eid al-adha (March 6, 2001) spoke at length about the nature of sacrifice in Abrahamic tradition but did not mention the Taliban or Afghanistan. A well-written essay on the editorial page of the same day pointed out the hypocrisy of the Taliban's concern with the "false gods" of dead stone at a time when the "false gods" of starvation, poverty, cruelty, sickness, unemployment, and ignorance were stronger every day, and for which no Mahmud of Ghazna seemed forthcoming.[26]

Jang's coverage of the events contrasts with that of other Urdu dailies, which reflected a point of view more divergent from the attitude of the international community. The popular Lahore-based daily *Nawa-i waqt* was openly supportive of the Taliban; the Sunday magazine of its March 18 issue ran a full-page article comparing how the suffering of children failed to move the West, while earthen statues brought out their "humanity."

Conclusion

The destruction of the Buddhas illustrates the vast gap that exists in the values and priorities of different populations within South Asian societies. Those who condemned the destruction of statues on the grounds of preservation of global heritage, art, and religious tolerance, view the icon smashers as the standard-bearers of an archaic ideology completely out of place in modern society. The defenders of the act of destruction see the condemners as dupes and apologists of the West, deracinated and desacralized.

The important question is whether it would have been possible to save the Buddha statues. It is conceivable that, had international sanctions on Afghanistan been lifted and combined with nonsensationalistic diplomatic efforts, the Taliban might have been convinced to let another country take custody of the statues. But in light of the Taliban's human-rights record and their stance on the extradition of bin Laden, there was little chance of a more conciliatory international position.

It is critical to note that the Taliban did not approach the crisis of the Bamiyan Buddhas with a preconceived plan. Not only did their position change over the weeks in question but so did their self-conception and their reputation among their wider base of sympathizers. What started out as a vague iconoclastic impulse became sharply focused as a reenactment of prophetic tradition, the Abrahamic precedent being invoked not just in the iconoclastic act but also in the symbolism of sacrifice, since the deaths of children as a direct consequence of international sanctions evoked Abraham's willingness to sacrifice his child for his monotheistic God. Their understanding of Muslim doctrine concerning religious figural imagery evolved through their response to international offers to remove the artifacts or of screening them in such a way that passersby could not see them: not only did the Taliban come to see the statues' presence in Afghanistan as a threat, but they also came to fear that any willingness to allow the Buddhas to survive in another country would make themselves complicit in perpetuating idolatry. And finally, linking the Buddhas to the Babri Mosque recast the traditionally isolationist Taliban as part of an international Muslim movement, since the destruction of the mosque was important to Muslims in Pakistan and India but had little resonance in Afghanistan. Their internationalization was recognized when both Chechen separatists and Kashmiri militants expressed support for the Taliban's actions. In the end, their actions were seen as meeting with divine approval in the widely circulated reports of drought-ending rain immediately following the destruction of the statues.[27]

The events of February and March 2001 confirmed the Taliban's status in the eyes of their supporters as pious champions of Islam against its international foes, just as it reaffirmed the view of the international community (and this includes the majority of Muslims) that the Taliban were intolerant, uneducated, and irrational. The current government of Afghanistan has declared rebuilding the Bamiyan Buddhas a cultural imperative, although it remains unclear when and how this will be carried out. One of the more ambitious schemes approved by the government is a proposal by the Japanese artist Hiro Yamagata to mount a sound-and-laser show that would project Buddha images at Bamiyan, powered by hundreds of windmills that would also supply electricity to surrounding residents. The cost is estimated at $64 million.[28] Many people have questioned the ethics of spending large sums to make replica statues in a country where the overwhelming majority of the population lives without personal security or the basic necessities of life. The moral balance of human lives against inanimate artifacts faced with destruction is difficult to weigh—and the dilemma is no easier when considering their reconstruction.

Author Biography
Jamal J. Elias is professor of religious studies at the University of Pennsylvania, where he holds the Class of 1965 Term Professorship in the School of Arts and Sciences. He is the author of a number of books and articles on a wide range of subjects dealing with Islamic cultural and intellectual history.

Endnotes
An earlier version of this essay was presented at the conference Deus (e)X Historia: Exploring Divinity and Reason in the Production of Knowledge, held at the Massachusetts Institute of Technology in April 2007.
[1] Finbarr Barry Flood, "Between Cult and Culture: Bamiyan, Islamic Iconoclasm, and the Museum," *The Art Bulletin* 84, no. 4 (December 2002): 641–59. Flood's essay also contains a very thoughtful discussion of questions of museumship and preservation as they pertain to the international attempt to preserve the Buddhas of Bamiyan.
[2] Zahiruddin Muhammad Babur Mirza, *Bâburnâma (Chaghatay Turkish Text with Abdul-Rahim Khankhanan's Persian Translation)*, ed. and trans. by W. M. Thackston Jr., Sources of Oriental Languages and Literatures 18 (Cambridge: Department of Near Eastern Languages and Civilizations, Harvard University, 1993), 3:728–29.
[3] Al-Muqaddasi, *The Best Divisions for Knowledge of the Regions (Ahsan al-taqāsim fī ma'rifat al-aqālīm)*, trans. Basil Collins (Reading, UK: Garnet, 2001), 390.
[4] Ibn al-Kalbi, *The Book of Idols (Kitāb al-asnām)*, trans. N. Amin Faris (Princeton, N.J.: Princeton University Press, 1969), 21–22. This version of the destruction of al-'Uzza is not found in the collections of Prophetic traditions *(hadith)* considered canonical by the majority of Muslims, but notions of canonicity have little bearing on the construction of sacred history, or on the impact such narratives have on attitudes toward art, objects, or much else. There is a large corpus of prophetic traditions that serve as the wisdom literature of Muslims, guiding attitudes and ethics in all walks of life.
[5] Detailed information on various reactions to this decree and other related events is available at the Archeological Institute of America's Web site, http://www.archaeology.org/online/news/afghanistan/index.htm.
[6] "Taliban to Implement Edict on the Destruction of Statues," *Pakistan Times*, February 28, 2001.
[7] "Taliban Assembling Explosives to Blow up Buddha Statues," *Pakistan Times*, March 3, 2001.

[8] "Taliban Leader Defends Afghan Statue Destruction," *Pakistan Times* (Reuters), March 6, 2001.

[9] "Taliban Resume Bamiyam Buddhas' Destruction," *Pakistan Times*, March 10, 2001.

[10] "No Shift in Policy on Osama, Statues: Taliban," *Pakistan Times*, March 16, 2001.

[11] "Taliban Assure Protection to Historic Relics," *Pakistan Times*, March 20, 2001.

[12] Molly Moore, "Afghanistan's Antiquities under Assault," *Washington Post Foreign Service*, Friday, March 2, 2001.

[13] "UN Condemns Taleban on Statues," *BBC News*, March 2, 2001: http://news.bbc.co.uk/1/hi/world/south_asia/1210927.stm. According to the report, the claim was made by the UN coordinator for Afghanistan.

[14] Jean-Michel Frodon, "The War of Images, or the Bāmiyān Paradox," in *iconoclash: Beyond the Image Wars in Science, Religion, and Art,* ed. B. Latour and P. Weibel, 221–23 (Karlsruhe and Cambridge, Mass.: ZKM and MIT Press, 2002), 222.

[15] Jean-François Clément, "The Empty Niche of the Bāmiyān Buddha," in *iconoclash: Beyond the Image Wars in Science, Religion, and Art,* ed. B. Latour and P. Weibel, 218–20 (Karlsruhe and Cambridge, Mass.: ZKM and MIT Press, 2002), 218.

[16] The question of why the Taliban did not destroy the Buddhas earlier in their rule of Bamiyan remains unanswered. Their anger at having been internationally ostracized no doubt played a role. It is also likely that different factions within the Taliban disagreed on how artifacts from Afghanistan's pre-Islamic past should be treated, with Mullah Umar representing the tolerant end of the spectrum (evidenced by his declaration of protection in 1999) and hard-liners, such as Mullah Dadullah (killed in May 2007), insisting on their destruction from the beginning and eventually leaving Umar with no choice in the matter.

[17] For an introduction to the Taliban and their relationship with the Pakistani government and society, see Ahmed Rashid, *Taliban: Militant Islam, Oil, and Fundamentalism in Central Asia* (New Haven, Conn.: Yale University Press, 2001).

[18] A. Rajagopal, *Politics after Television: Hindu Nationalism and the Reshaping of the Public in India* (Cambridge: Cambridge University Press, 2001). See also V. Naregal, *Language Politics, Elites, and the Public Sphere* (New Delhi: Permanent Black, 2001) and R. Jeffrey, *India's Newspaper Revolution: Capitalism, Politics, and the Indian-Language Press, 1977–99* (New York: St. Martin's Press, 2000). The Babri Mosque, named after the aforementioned emperor Babur, commemorates the establishment of Mughal rule and is viewed with reverence by many South Asian Muslims.

[19] The letters were: Barkatullah Marwat (Kuwait), March 15, 2001; A. Khan (Islamabad) March 28, 2001; Rohul Amin (Swat), March 30, 2001.

The United States of America imposed unilateral financial and economic sanctions on the Taliban on July 5, 1999, in an attempt to force them to stop providing sanctuary to Osama bin Laden. On October 15 of the same year the UN Security Council unanimously adopted Resolution 1267, which imposed financial sanctions and a flight-ban on Taliban-controlled Afghanistan if it failed to turn bin Laden over to a competent authority within thirty days. These sanctions were strengthened in December 2000, despite an August 2000 report from the UN Office for the Coordination of Humanitarian Affairs (OCHA) that the sanctions were having "tangible negative effect" on the population of Afghanistan ("Sanctions against Al Qaeda and the Taliban," *Global Policy Forum:* http://www.globalpolicy.org/security/sanction/indexafg.htm.).

[20] "Ye Bābrī Masjid kī shahādat kā radd-e 'amal hē, Tālibān" (This Is the Consequence of the Martyrdom of the Babri Mosque), *Jang,* March 5, 2001.

[21] This statement has gained much popularity among Muslim admirers of Mahmud of Ghazna, although it does not accurately reflect his words as they appear in the historical work from which they are drawn. The chronicle *Tārīkh-i firishta* describes Mahmud as being concerned with the judgment of posterity and declaring his preference for being remembered as a destroyer of idols. See Muhammad Qasim Firishta, *Tārīkh-e firishta,* 2 vols. (Lucknow, India: n.p., 1905), 1:33; English translation by John Briggs, *History of the Rise of the Mohammedan Power in India,* 4 vols. (1829; rpt. Delhi: Low Price Publications, 1990), 1:43–44).

[22] "Mullah 'Umar nē but-shikanī kā hukm dē kar sunnat-e Ibrāhīmī ko zinda kiyā" (Mullah Umar's Brings the Tradition of Abraham Back to Life by Ordering the Destruction of Idols), *Jang,* March 2, 2001.

[23] "Mullah 'Umar kī siyāsat nē maghrib kō hilā kar rakh diyā" (Mullah Umar's Strategy Leaves the West Shaken), *Jang,* March 5, 2001.

[24] "Tālibān nē butōn ko tor kar Nabī-ye Akram kī sunnat adā kī" (Taliban Fulfill the Tradition of the Noblest Prophet by Destroying Statues), *Jang,* March 11, 2001.

[25] "Afghanistan mēn but tōrnē kā iqdām durust hē" (Decision to Destroy Idols in Afghanistan Is Correct), *Jang*, March 6, 2001.

[26] Hasan Nisar, "But-shikanī kā shawq" (Fondness for Iconoclasm), *Jang*, March 6, 2001.

[27] "But tūtē to Afghanistan mēn bārish shurū' hō ga'ī" (When the Idols Broke Rain Began Falling in Afghanistan), *Nawa-i waqt,* March 10, 2001.

[28] Carlotta Gall, "Afghans Consider Rebuilding Bamiyan Buddhas," *International Herald Tribune,* December 5, 2006: http://www.iht.com/articles/2006/12/05/news/buddhas.php?page=1. For more on reconstruction plans, see "The Bamiyan Project": http://www.photogrammetry.ethz.ch/research/bamiyan/buddha/index.html.

1. Tugendhat House, Brno, Czech Republic. Constructed 1928–30. Photograph 2004, courtesy World Monuments Fund.

Catherine Ingraham

Takings

In a short guide on historic preservation law, the opening sentence reads: "Historic preservation and the law have been surprising but comfortable bedfellows for well over a century.... Most people are unaware of the complex array of legal tools that generally lie behind a particular site's rehabilitation or preservation."[1] The comfortable fit between preservation and law is, on the face of it, not at all surprising. Law and historic preservation emanate from the same institutional place, governmental legislation, and are bound by the same language, the "textual parsimony," of legal statutes.[2]

Insofar as historic preservation is a good thing, beneficial to culture as a whole and protective of cultural resources, it is good in the same sense that laws are good: laws adjudicate and smooth differences and synthesize, in practical ways, ideas of a common good. Laws allow us to live, somewhat as ourselves, in the midst of otherness. Historic preservation is not typically good in the sense that art is good; art emanates from personal expression and ruthlessly bares the question of the good to scrutiny.

On the other hand, because it is frequently involved with art and architecture, historic preservation's relation to law, and the language of the law, is precarious. One of preservation law's primary purposes is to protect against other actions emanating from its own civic and political base—city, state, federal government—that might damage or come into conflict with designated sites of preservation. It acts as an institutionalized homeopathy to government expansionism or avarice and is, therefore, itself always politically at risk.

Property owners who challenge historic preservation laws sometimes argue that "such laws... amount to a taking of private property." The term "taking" refers to the fifth amendment in the U.S. Constitution, which states: "nor shall private property be taken for public use without just compensation." Eminent domain originates in this amendment, as do aspects of historic preservation that come into conflict with private property. Private property is the privileged domain of common law in Western cultures, and when such property is "taken" it is also, in legal terms, "weakened."[3] In the United States, the right to property is understood, tacitly, as an originary entitlement, as powerful in its influence on public and private life as if it were one of those three, loudly enunciated, rights in the

Future Anterior
Volume IV, Number 2
Winter 2007

Declaration of Independence: "life, liberty, and the pursuit of happiness."[4] It is the unstated guarantor for "rights" as a juridical—and, more specifically, biojuridical—idea.

In takings cases, the Supreme Court has ruled that there must be "an essential nexus between the burdens placed on the property owners and a legitimate state interest affected by the proposed development. In other words, there should be a reasonable correlation between the conditions placed on the property owner and the public interest being served."[5] The words *nexus* and *correlation,* in this context, are quite interesting because they imply that private property, legally and hermeneutically, harbors negotiable principles based on both its alienable and inalienable character. Not only is most property alienable—able to be sold or given away—but it is also inalienable, able to be kept. I am not offering a political or ideological defense of private property but, instead, broadening the idea of private property to include an inalienable dimension. This will be, at best, a preliminary inclusion that certainly does not originate with me. But I want to open up an aspect of the subject slightly different from what historic preservation might typically bring to mind.

Maurice Godelier, an anthropologist working in the later part of the twentieth century, argued that there can be no human society without two domains: "the domain of *exchanges,* whatever is exchanged and whatever the form of this exchange . . . and the domain in which individuals and groups carefully *keep* for themselves, then transmit to their descendents or fellow-believers, things, narratives, names, forms of thinking."[6] Godelier was particularly interested in the problem of the gift—what is given and, in particular, what is kept rather than circulated in cultures. "Things that are kept," Godelier writes, "are always 'realities' which transport an individual or group back to another time, which place them once again before their origins, before the origin." These kept realities "give time its duration," he continues, and are "anchor points for the formation of individual and collective identities."[7]

Marcel Mauss observed in the 1930s that, in certain cultures, lodged in objects are souls. Mauss's theory was that there is something in a "thing given" that needs to return to its original owner. Thus, in human social systems, according to Mauss, there is an "obligation to give because giving creates obligation."[8] Godelier replaces Mauss's idea of soul with *rights.* Objects become attached to human beings through rights that may or may not be part of a written body of law and may or may not be alienable. Some objects are given as gifts, and when this happens, part of the rights of the original owner over the object, according to Godelier, travel with the gift.

We usually include, in the modern definition of property — whether taken, given, or sold — a potential for alienability such that a thing can be completely severed from its seller or giver and completely transferred to a buyer or receiver, with no remaining obligation. The power of property systems to corrupt, particularly private-property systems, is precisely the power of "alienability" to commodify everything and to act coldly, to sever relationships without any residue or obligation to restore them. Whether property is sold or given, some transfer of an object from one person to another is involved. However, gifts, in particular, engender a reciprocal dependence, an obligation that cannot be repaid in kind, and they follow, as Godelier argues, a "rule of law" that binds both giver and object:

> Coming back to Mauss's second question, if there is some power in the thing, it is essentially that of the relationship which binds it to the person of the giver. This is a twofold relationship since the giver continues to be present in the thing given, which does not become detached from his [physical or legal] person, and this presence is a force, that of the rights he continues to exercise *over the thing given* and through it *over the recipient* who accepts it. In accepting a gift, one accepts more than a thing, one accepts the fact that the giver has rights over the receiver.[9]

In Western law, it is more difficult to see how things carry rights because, unlike kinship cultures such as those studied by Mauss, "people" and "things" are divided into separate systems.[10] Mauss, Godelier argues, does not "take into account the fact that it is not only personal presence [that is, a spiritual quality in a thing that, in the cultures he studied, was regarded as a person and acted as one], but also *rights* that leave with the object in question."[11] And it is these rights that make an object valuable, as property, when it is removed from circulation. Godelier suggests that Mauss' avoidance of analyzing gift giving in culture from the "standpoint of the notion of inalienable property" — property that is not taken, given, or sold but kept — was related to "chaotic discussions that had surrounded the notions of collective and individual ownership since the end of the nineteenth century."[12] In Godelier's work, as already intimated, what is kept is also a kind of property and, he further claims, this kept property ensures the circulation of other kinds of things and people.

Historic preservation — which works inside both legal and economic structures — frequently takes alienable property and makes it inalienable by, in effect, depositing objects inside a cultural vault.[13] Thus are we placed before our "origins" —

"beginnings," as Edward Said called them—that include both historical and genealogical dimensions. Politically, preservation is interested in stabilizing culture around generational, as well as historical, values—which often accounts for its conservative position. Because a correlation is required between what an owner will lose, and his or her compensation in the form of a public gain, historic preservation must make the case—particularly in architectural restorations—that there is a commensurate, or compensatory, value in isolating the kept aspect of property from its exchange potential. Nexus arguments almost always lean on philosophical conceptions of the "common good," which refer to historical ideas, generic humanisms, and, in ways less easily tracked, the exercise of aesthetic judgment.

By way of a conclusion—in this very broad array of proposals that are radically inconclusive at this stage—I want to briefly look at the architectural restoration of the Tugendhat House. This house was not given as a gift but taken in the property melee that ensued after World War II. My discussion, therefore, concerns what is taken and then kept, not what is given or kept from being given. Godelier's remarks have, accordingly, a limited bearing on this example, but the transmission of rights in the transfer of objects is germane to the peculiar web of architectural, bio-juridical, and property rights issues within which the house is now caught.

The Tugendhat House in Brno, Czech Republic, designed by Mies van der Rohe and Lilly Reich in the 1920s, has recently been in the news.[14] Heirs of the Tugendhat family, who fled from Brno in 1938, are attempting to recover the house from the city in order to supervise a badly needed restoration. During the war, the house was occupied by the Gestapo and, later, the Messerschmidt aircraft factory office, and, even later, by the Russian Calvary. After the war, it served for a time as a school of modern rhythm and dance and was then "nationalized" and appropriated by the government. It served then as a rehabilitation department of the local Children's Hospital. In the early 1960s, the villa was renovated and listed as a culturally significant building.[15] Laws governing the return of property to its rightful owners, as part of the War Reparations Act, expired in 1995. It is thus too late for the Tugendhat family to reclaim the house under reparations. In order to justify the return of the house, the family is standing on moral grounds, although nothing has yet been settled in favor of, or against, them.[16] The Tugendhats' lawyers are arguing that the house was an artwork stolen from the family and implicitly, perhaps, that the family would be better curators of the house's restoration than the city.

Property transactions, smooth or disputed, often reveal incomplete histories—in this case, the history of postwar communism in Brno and the history of the Tugendhat family. Ethical and juridical structures are activated by the transfer of property partly because property is, by definition, owned by people. It is not a denatured thing. The legal scholar Joseph William Singer defines property as the "relations among people with regard to things."[17] Because the Tugendhat house is a World Heritage Site and an architectural icon—"studied by every architectural student," as Barry Bergdoll has stated[18]—we might also ask whether the architectural meaning of the house, which is sunk into its property meaning, belongs primarily to "relations among people" (family, government, historians, students) or to "things" (the "architectural house" designed and built in Brno). This question cannot be entirely satisfied by a historical account of events or legal arguments.

The Roman natural historian Pliny the Elder (first century AD) might have seen, in the various transfers of the Tugendhat House from family to Nazis to Russians to city, not the direct expression of architectural issues, property rights, or world politics, but a story of failed proprieties in a particular family. He might have seen the family as failing to act according to genealogical laws, which would entail—in Pliny's simultaneously fundamentalist and expansive world—a particular relationship to the artistic objects under its care. The city of Brno is suggesting something similar. The family apparently recently sold a Wilhelm Lehmbruck statue, "Torso of a Walking Women," a replica of which now stands in the house, for two million dollars at Sotheby's.[19] The city is suggesting that the sale of this original statue indicates that the family does not have the house, as an "original historical" entity, foremost in its thoughts.

Pliny was working, as the art historian Georges Didi-Huberman writes, in a more open epistemic field than we normally attribute to art history. Included under the heading of "art" were medicine, agriculture, and a multitude of practices and things that Pliny explores in his *Natural History.* In his world, art occurs "every time people use, instrumentalize, imitate, or go beyond nature."[20] Very little of this art is based on aesthetic evaluation, which, Didi-Huberman argues, is a key difference between Pliny's antique theory of art and Vasari's Renaissance theory of art, from which our modern theory of art is precipitated. Pliny's theory of representation refers to what he calls "barren" matter that "relates to the natural world, that is to say, to life"[21]—"brute materials" such as metal and rocks, and artisanal activities such as engraving, molding, and dyeing. His temporality is that of biology as it is distilled through genealogical lines. "Historical *teleology,* which will be Vasari's prime concern," Didi-Huberman argues, is opposed to a "*genealogy* of the image and of resemblance, which Pliny expresses in terms of law, justice, and right."[22] By "imago," images, he means not paintings but molded wax likenesses of heroic ancestors. These were kept in niches in one's house, in a family archive. "Outside the house and in its doorway, there would be other representations of these [ancestors] . . . with spoils taken from the enemy fastened to them, which even those who subsequently bought the house were not permitted to unfasten. Thus the house would celebrate for eternity, and irrespective of changes in ownership, the triumphs of those that had lived there."[23] A family house, in Pliny's terms, was meant to house the aggregation of a family's ancestral life. This "anthropology of resemblance" could be just or unjust, legal or illegal, and took its legitimacy "from a juridical space on the boundary of public and private law."[24]

In Pliny's terms, one could argue that the Tugendhat family was both not free and free to sell Wilhelm Lehmbruck's statue, which, in a larger sense, stood for the possibility of recovering the house as a genealogical object in spite of the massive damage it had sustained from its temporary occupations during and after the war. The statue, if it authentically belongs to the furnishings of the house (damaged furnishings that will require meticulous restoration), would be part of what a historic preservationist would attempt to keep in the house in order to dramatize a particular historic moment in the development of architectural modernism.

But the family was also free to sell the statue because it had been given to them, they owned it, and it was detachable and, therefore, alienable property. In addition, in Pliny's terms, the woman depicted in the "Torso" represented a "stranger," who bore no resemblance to any members of the Tugendhat family. It was an idealized sculpture of a human form that could be seen as an "unjust" work of art that had no place in the house to begin with.

I am not making a legal or aesthetic judgment of any kind about what should happen in this case, since I am neither a lawyer nor do I know all the details of the case. My interest, instead, is to bring to mind, when we think of architecture and, in this case, a restoration of an iconographic house, certain questions of rights—historical and genealogical—that are residual in property and might be activated by property transfers or disputes such as those taking place around the Tugendhat House. And my further interest is to explore how inalienable property, *kept* property, sequesters these rights in a particular way that, if Godelier is correct, allows other objects and relations among people to circulate.

Georges Didi-Huberman is an art historian and does not, therefore, seem particularly struck by the spectacle of a house filled with wax molds of people's heads adorned with war fetishes preserved in niches in the walls. But Pliny's examples of the failure of art to act "legally" are almost all architectural in character. One of the most virulent transgressions of genealogical law, according to Pliny, is a cultivation of *luxuria,* an excess of materials, which is the very definition of architecture after Vasari. Architecture *is* excess, it exists over and above mere building, thickens and makes more extravagant, and artificial, the use of materials. It also claims transcendental meanings. Didi-Huberman notes Pliny's objections to the "'moral insanity' of 'carrying the entrails of the earth—marble—into their bedrooms.'"[25] Gilded walls are "obscenities" of precious metals and are "portraits of money" that, to Pliny, are incidents of *permutatio.*[26] *Permutatio* refers to the loss of the dignity and tradition of generational transmission—resemblances that touch, literally, the face of the subject and natural laws that control the passage of objects from one person to the next. These have been replaced, Pliny complains, by "exchange, of commerce, of money."[27] The conservative, severely delimited aspects of Pliny's oppositions frame larger relations between conceptions of temporal continuity—generational structures connected through time and space—and what we now define as a temporal discontinuity of time and space, that is, history. Generational logic is based on an implacable system of biological heredity and reproduction, which Pliny theorizes into natural law, and historical logic is based on epistemology, teleology, and a broad conception of culture.

We can see, in the arguments surrounding the Tugendhat house, and in the house itself, influences from both of these logics. The human figuration of Lehmbruck's statute already mentioned, the use of natural stone and natural wood, the interior and exterior openness of the living room, and the fact that we refer to the house as the "Tugendhat House," contribute to the manner in which the house is closely, like most architectural houses, bound to some natural history of a family from which all the events that transpire in the house over its history have emanated. Simultaneously, the house is inseparable from its historical context, both architecturally and politically. An art market exists; art exists in the form of the "excess" of architectural beauty and rich materials; the house is a piece of property.

The final paragraph of the *New York Times* article states that, in spite of the contentious battles between city authorities and family authorities, the city sees cooperation with the family as a "long-term thing." These words are uttered as if to say, in a weary tone, "there is no getting rid of the family," as if we had, in fact, found a way out of our own genealogical time and space, through modernism, only to be drawn back through the very things and actions that had seemed to liberate us — the practices of art, architecture, science, progressive ideas of culture, notions of public and urban life, teleological history.

Author Biography
Catherine Ingraham has lectured and published widely in architecture and architectural history and theory. Dr. Ingraham is currently professor of architecture in the Graduate Architecture Department at Pratt Institute in New York City, a program of which she was chair from 1998 to 2005. Her publications include her most recent book, *Architecture, Animal, Human: The Asymmetrical Condition* (2006), *Architecture and The Burdens of Linearity* (1998), and numerous articles, essays, and chapters in journals and books.

Endnotes
[1] Julia H. Miller, *A Layperson's Guide to Historic Preservation Law: A Survey of Federal, State, and Local Laws Governing Historic Resource Protection* (Washington, D.C.: National Trust for Historic Preservation, 2000), 1.
[2] Costas Douzinas and Lynda Nead, eds., *Law and the Image: The Authority of Art and the Aesthetics of Law* (Chicago: The University of Chicago Press, 1999), 3.
[3] Ibid., 2
[4] In the formation of the United States, and in spite of an abiding belief in principles of the public good, private property always was, and still is, the "privileged domain of common law." This is often seen as evidence of the strong influence of John Locke's theories of property and revolution had on the drafting of the American Constitution.
[5] Miller, *A Layperson's Guide,* 25.
[6] Maurice Godelier, *The Enigma of the Gift* (Chicago: The University of Chicago Press, 1999), 200; author's emphasis
[7] Ibid., 200–201.
[8] Ibid., 15.
[9] Ibid., 44–45. Claude Lévi-Strauss, the structural anthropologist, replaced Mauss's mystical idea of some "soul of the giver" in a thing, which occasions its return to its source, with the more universal characterization of culture and society as a kinship system based on exchange. Exchange is not optional, according to Lévi-Strauss, but part of linguistic and unconscious mental structures to which institutions give us access. Symbolic systems are articulated by these unconscious

mental structures" and, for Lévi-Strauss, "symbols are more real than what they signify" (23–27).

[10] Godelier, *Enigma*, 46. One can see this explicitly in William Blackstone's first treatises on law.

[11] Ibid., 46–47.

[12] Ibid., 46

[13] Through the tax structure, as we know, the gift, in American philanthropic culture, has been the very basis of the transfer from corporate life of part of its profits to cultural life. The word *vault* may seem histrionic but it is accurate.

[14] Jim Rendon, "A Mies Masterwork, Deteriorating and in Dispute," *New York Times,* March 22, 2007.

[15] *The Villa of the Tugendhats Created by Mies van der Rohe in Brno,* (published by the Institute for the Protection of Monuments in Brno, Brno City Museum, 1995).

[16] "The city says it recognizes the family's moral right to the home, and the family says it wants to keep it open for the people of the city, but neither side seems to trust the other's ability to manage the restoration work and maintenance that will be necessary" (Rendon, "A Mies Masterwork").

[17] Joseph William Singer, *Introduction to Property* (New York: Aspen, 2005), 2.

[18] Bergdoll made this remark in Rendon's "A Mies Masterwork."

[19] "Daniela Hammer-Tugendhat, the youngest daughter of the original owners, Fritz and Grete Tugendhat, is well aware of the house's significance. An art history professor at the University of Applied Arts in Vienna, she has spent much of her life trying to make sure that it is properly cared for. . . . Though she never lived in the house—she was born in Venezuela after the war—it has become her obsession. For decades, she and her husband, Ivo Hammer, a professor of conservation at the University of Applied Sciences and Arts in Hildensheim, Germany, and a restorer of murals, petitioned the Communist and then post-Communist governments to have it opened to the public and then to have it properly restored" (Rendon, "A Mies Masterwork").

[20] Georges Didi-Huberman, "The Molding Image," in *Law and the Image,* 73.

[21] Ibid., 74.

[22] Ibid., 76

[23] "The family tree" would also be "traced in lines on the wall" (ibid., 78).

[24] Ibid., 79–80

[25] Ibid., 81.

[26] Ibid.

[27] Ibid., 84.

1. Leopoldo Torres Balbás in the Alhambra, Granada, Spain. Photograph courtesy of Patronato de la Alhambra y el Generalife.

Juan Calatrava

Leopoldo Torres Balbás
Architectural Restoration and the Idea of "Tradition" in Early Twentieth-Century Spain

The process of revision of contemporary architectural history set in motion some decades ago has not only revealed a rich and complex panorama that is not reducible to linear and teleological accounts, but it has also allowed us to finally place in the context of this historical landscape episodes and figures that had until recently received only local or marginal attention. That is precisely the situation of Leopoldo Torres Balbás (1888–1960)[1]—an architect, conservator, architectural and urban historian, and theoretician of architectural restoration and historic preservation—who has now emerged as one of the key figures of Spanish architectural discourse in the first half of the twentieth century.

In 1916, when Torres Balbás published his first text, that architectural discourse was framed by a wide cultural polemic, which sought to define what "Spanish architecture" stood for and what its basic referents should be. The question of defining the essence of "Spanishness" was a key theme in Hispanic culture at the end of the nineteenth century and the beginning of twentieth. The crisis of 1898, after war with the United States and the loss of Cuba and the Philippines, proved the urgency for modernization in Spain. But numerous intellectuals of what would later be known as the *Generación del 98* (that is, Azorín, Ramiro de Maeztu, Joaquin Costa or, above all, Miguel de Unamuno, whose thoughts on the relationship between modernity and tradition were fundamental for Torres Balbás) understood this modernization not so much in terms of a radical rupture with the past but as a return to the true roots of history and of popular tradition. Architects, having exhausted the expressive possibilities of nineteenth-century historicism, gave attention to the peculiar "mosaic" of Spanish villages and favored the blossoming of regionalisms. However, already by 1918–20, architects and intellectuals alike, from Torres Balbás to Federico García Lorca, were becoming critical of regionalism as nothing but a folklorist pastiche. In this context, Torres Balbás's theories assumed a fundamental role: the revalorization of the idea of *tradition* and the difficult attempt to make the authentic roots of the popular compatible with modernity.

Leopoldo Torres Balbás was born in Madrid, the son of a geographer father, who instilled in him a passion for travel. He entered the Madrid School of Architecture in 1910 and

Future Anterior
Volume IV, Number 2
Winter 2007

graduated in 1916. On top of his architectural studies, he always remained tied to the Institución Libre de Enseñanza (Free Institution of Education), a foundation that pioneered secular, progressive, and high-culture education in Spain.[2] He was also a student in the archaeology department of the Centro de Estudios Históricos (Center for Historical Studies), then under the directorship of Manuel Gómez Moreno, one of the founders of twentieth-century Spanish art historiography. Both of these institutions gave Torres Balbás a solid education in history and archeology, and an ideology that would prove decisive in reviewing Spanish architectural history: the importance of travel as a way of acquiring knowledge and as a pedagogical tool. Thus, he inscribed himself in the tradition of those great travelers, who from the time of Antonio Ponz and the Romantic writers and artists had traveled across Spain creating an inventory of its artistic and architectural treasures.

Torres Balbás inserted the exaltation of travel into the preoccupations of the *Generación del 98,* finding the "Deep Spain," which for them constituted the true soul of the country. Throughout his many voyages, Torres Balbás was able to catalog and bring to light buildings that would have otherwise disappeared. It is not by chance that the outbreak of the Civil War in 1936 took him by surprise in Soria, where he had gone on a study trip with his students and where he was forced to stay for the three years of the conflict.

One aspect of Torres Balbás' early career as an architect, which has been overshadowed by his work as conservator, is the fact that he was a key figure in the journal *Arquitectura,* the official publication of Spanish architects and the main forum of architectural debate during the 1920s and 1930s.[3] He was secretary of the journal from 1918 to 1923, and from its pages he was able to shape the forms and methods of architectural criticism in Spain, the absence of which Torres Balbás considered a sign of intolerable cultural backwardness.[4] Most importantly, his articles, eighteen of which appeared under the general rubric of "Arquitectura española contemporánea" (Spanish Contemporary Architecture), opened the door for public debate on contemporary architecture for the first time in Spain. In his writings one can find, negatively expressed, a desire for architecture to be modern, not through blind rupture but precisely for knowing both how to look at the past with new eyes and how to incorporate anonymous secular memory into the demands of the contemporary city.

Torres Balbás hardly practiced architecture professionally, but two of his rare works are related to Granada, the city where the ideas put forth in his writings would end up taking root. We will later return to his role as conservator of the Alhambra, but it was in Granada where he collaborated with Antonio

Flórez on the construction of the Escuela Normal (Normal School) and where he imagined the Granada Pavilion for the Iberoamerican Exhibition of Seville of 1929. The former especially proves the common interest of Flórez and Torres Balbás to base their designs on the use of traditional materials, in this case brick, and the construction methods employed in vernacular architecture. Torres Balbás's interest in popular architecture was crystallized in many publications, among them *La vivienda popular en España* (Popular Housing in Spain) of 1933, and must be understood as an attempt to bridge tradition and modernity, a constant theme of all his writings, beginning with one of his first articles, "Mientras labran los sillares" (While They Dress Ashlars).[5]

Popular architecture offered Spanish architects is a way to renew architecture through simplicity, ornamental austerity, and sincerity of construction. These same features can be found in Torres Balbás's writings on Spanish architectural history. For example, Torres's analysis of the Escorial Monastery, the mythic building of Spanish architecture par excellence, described the design as a conflict between learned architecture, "with contempt towards our history and our race," and a living tradition, "buried and silent" within the people. This tradition is expressed in the toughness and austerity of a building that "pretends to be classical and European yet only manages to resemble one of those torn off, granite boulders, in the mountains for thousands of years."[6]

One cannot detach Torres Balbas's position within the contemporary architectural debate from his thinking and practice in heritage conservation and architectural restoration, which are the best-known aspects of his work. Since the end of the nineteenth century, the criterion for monumental restoration had been under debate in Spain, and the so-called stylistic restoration, based on Viollet-le-Duc's theories and the idea of the "unity" of the monument, had come increasingly into question.[7] At the Sixth National Congress of Architects, held in Madrid in 1904, this subject was chosen as one of the topics for debate. The most important among the defenders of Violletian ideas was undoubtedly Vicente Lampérez y Romea, a prestigious architect and author of important works of architectural history.[8] Lampérez restored both cathedrals in Cuenca and Burgos, where he completely reconstructed the façade of the former and isolated the latter. Although he did criticize the fantasizing excesses of Viollet-le-Duc's disciples more that once, the truth is that Lampérez clearly aligned himself with interventionist restoration and with the attempt to give back to the monument an original image, which was not always based on rigorous historical and archaeological knowledge.

The confrontation between the Spanish Violettian and Ruskinian schools took place in 1919, at the Seventh National Congress of Architects held in Saragossa and chaired by Lampérez himself. The young Torres Balbás spoke on "Legislación, inventario gráfico y organización de los Monumentos históricos y artísticos de España" (Legislation, graphical archive, and organization of Spanish historical and artistic monuments). He outlined the main arguments for a new way of engaging the remains of the past: "To preserve buildings just as they have been passed on to us, to protect them from the ruin, to maintain them and consolidate them, always with great respect toward the ancient construction; never to complete them or remake the existent parts."[9] Against stylistic restoration he set an emphasis on conservation and a demand for maximum historical and archeological rigor before undertaking any intervention. Moreover Torres Balbás was one of the first to stress that the best guarantee for the conservation of historic buildings was to put them to modern use through activities compatible with their essence.

Torres Balbás would have numerous occasions to bring these principles into practice. His interventions on historical monuments were always accompanied by publications and studies of their architectural history. His trajectory had two climaxes: in 1923, when he was appointed preservation architect of the Alhambra in Granada; and 1929, when he became chief architect of the National Artistic Treasure and was in charge of a wide region that included all southeastern Spain, which allowed him to extend his field of work. In 1931 he took part in the renowned congress from which the Athens Charter was drafted. The document had wide circulation thanks to its publication both in the French journal *Mouseion* and, in a revised version later on, in *Arquitectura*.[10] In Athens, Torres Balbás could have met Gustavo Giovannoni, a figure with whom he had fundamental differences (among others, political) but with whom he also agreed in some points, such as the critique of the isolation of historical buildings.[11]

Torres Balbás served as preservation architect of the Alhambra from 1923 until 1936. This Andalusian city had a fundamental impact on his thinking. Shortly after his arrival he wrote *Granada, la ciudad que desaparece* (Granada, the Disappearing City), a text of great significance that called for the safeguard of historical memory as part of the modern growth of cities.[12] The thirteen years that Torres Balbás was in charge of the Alhambra proved absolutely decisive for its conservation and study. Following the ideas that Ricardo Velázquez Bosco, another pioneer of new restoration, had presented in the plan of 1917, Torres Balbás applied a new working model to the Alhambra, defined in his own words as "Not trying to

2. The Alhambra: the east wing of the Courtyard of the Lions, circa 1880. Photograph courtesy of Patronato de la Alhambra y el Generalife.

reproduce one part or element of ancient times, neither removing nor altering any testimonies from the past, respecting the works subsequently added to the first construction process; purely concerned with consolidation, sustainability, and preservation."[13]

His *Diario de Obras* (Construction Diary) of the Alhambra logged the enormous work undertaken and partly undermines his ideal of pure conservation of the existing fabric. Torres Balbás had to develop two types of intervention that are responsible for the present look of the monument. On one hand, the restoration of greatly degraded spaces involved the replacement of the original room with new elements recalling the original space but with modern materials. Such was the case in the Patio de las Damas (Courtyard of the Ladies) in the Palacio del Partal (Partal Palace) and in the southern gallery of the Patio de Machuca (Machuca Courtyard), which, although entirely missing, was evoked with topiaries. On the other hand, Torres Balbás did not extend his deference for subsequent additions to the interventions by nineteenth-century conservators steeped in Orientalist aesthetics, which he viewed as absolutely arbitrary. There, Torres Balbás did not hesitate to "restore the restored," that is, to remove some of those fantasizing additions.

This provoked rage of those elites in Granada who had become habituated to the Orientalist image of the Alhambra. The climax of this debate came in 1934 when Torres Balbás decided to remove the ceramic, polychromatic small domes with which Contreras had covered the small temple-like

pavilion on the eastern side of the Patio de los Leones (Courtyard of the Lions) in 1859, and replaced them with a simple, four-sloped ceiling designed on the basis of a rigorous historical study and comparative analysis of Islamic architecture of northern Africa. The magnitude of the controversy provoked of a group of intellectuals to publish a joint letter in support of Torres Balbás. These figures would later see their destinies unraveled by the civil war. Among them were the musician Manuel de Falla, instigator of the letter and exiled from 1939 onward; Antonio Gallego Burin, who became the first mayor of Granada under Franco; and Francisco Prieto Moreno, Torres's successor as the head of the Alhambra. The antagonism toward Torres Balbás found a direct path to action in the political changes precipitated by the civil war. When Franco took Granada on August 25, 1936, the city's new military officer removed Torres Balbás from his office as head of the Alhambra, "for being a person affect to the leftist regime." He escaped an almost certain death because, at the time, he was in Soria with his students.

In 1931 Torres Balbás earned the Chair of History of Architecture in the Madrid School of Architecture. Until 1936 he had been able to teach and carry out his tasks in the Alhambra

simultaneously, but his dismissal as preservation architect of Granada's monument drove him definitively into teaching and research. Once the Civil War ended he almost lost his chair in one of the purges to which Franco subjected public officials. Although he was able to keep his position in extremis, in practice he was prevented from any post or professional activity in the field of historic preservation. Despite personal grief, this new phase of forced withdrawal was essential for the development of modern architectural historiography in Spain. With the compound background of an exhaustive and direct knowledge of Spanish architecture and a reworked concept of "tradition," Torres Balbás published, throughout the 1940s and 1950s until his death in 1960, dozens of works on architectural history. These included publication reviews, monographic articles, especially on Islamic architecture, and several books, among them two volumes[14] for the collection *Ars Hispaniae* and, first and foremost his monumental and posthumous work *Ciudades hispanomusulmanas* of 1970, still an essential reference.[15]

With his lectures and publications, Torres Balbás trained a whole generation of architectural historians in a methodological model of historiography that, even considering essential the knowledge of documents, broke with the excessive mystification that historiographical positivism had placed in archival work. Although he considered archival work necessary, he did not think it alone was adequate to the requirements for writing architectural history. To the archive he added travel and the critical, personal, and direct knowledge of buildings in their contexts. The relevance he gave to architectural analysis turned the monument itself into a document. He upheld a philosophy of history in which architecture was nothing but the translation of that "true" Spain

5. Courtyard and tower of the Partal immediately after restoration. Photograph courtesy of Patronato de la Alhambra y el Generalife.

he thought had been hidden under historicist tinsel and folkloric frivolity.

Torres Balbás's legacy was carried forth by Fernando Chueca Goitia, undoubtedly his best disciple. Through Torres Balbás's teaching, Chueca connected with the set of problems of the *Generación del 98*—that is, the relationship between history and tradition—and he became largely responsible for the renewal of Spanish architectural historiography from 1940 on. Indeed, in 1952 Chueca convened a meeting in Granada of modern architects to collectively reflect on the future of Spanish architecture. They chose the Alhambra as the setting. What resulted from that meeting was the renowned *Manifiesto de la Alambra* (Alhambra's Manifesto), a programmatic text that called for a cautious modernity, one anchored in the tradition the Alhambra represented, not seen through Orientalist eyes but rather though the glance of architects in searching for "timeless" abstract lessons about volume and space in the Nasrid monument.[16] Torres Balbás was not present in the Alhambra meeting: the man who had done the most for the monument's preservation and for advancing scientific knowledge about the Alhambra had been ignominiously expelled from it in 1936. His ideas were, nevertheless, the ones beating within the pages of the *Manifesto*.

Author Biography

Juan Calatrava is an architectural historian who was also trained as a lawyer. He is professor of architectural history at Granada's Escuela Técnica Superior de Arquitectura, where he also serves as associate director of the school. He is author of five books and more than sixty articles on the history of architecture from the eighteenth to the twentieth century, as well as on the historiography and theory of architecture.

Endnotes

Translated by María González-Pendás.

[1] On Torres Balbás, see C. Vilchez, *La Alhambra de Leopoldo Torres Balbás* (Granada: Editorial Comares, 1988); monographic number in *Cuadernos de la Alhambra* 25 (1989); C. Vílchez, *Leopoldo Torres Balbás* (Granada: Editorial Comares, 1999); A. Muñoz Cosme, *La vida y la obra de Leopoldo Torres Balbás* (Seville: Consejería de Cultura de la Junta de Andalucía, 2005). Torres Balbás's more than two hundred texts have been gathered, if in an incomplete manner, in the nine volumes of his *Obra dispersa* (Madrid: Colegio Oficial de Arquitectos de Madrid, 1981–85). A good anthology of his main texts is Torres Balbás, *Sobre monumentos y otros escritos* (Madrid: Colegio Oficial de Arquitectos de Madrid, 1996).

[2] See, among a wide bibliography, the monographic number the *Institución Libre de Enseñanza*, no. 18–19 (1978) devoted to the journal *Poesía.*

[3] See the catalog for the exhibition *Revista Arquitectura (1918–1936)* (Madrid: Colegio Oficial de Arquitectos de Madrid y Ministerio de Fomento, 2001).

[4] "There is no architectural critique in our country. Modern painting and sculpture get discussed; hardly ever does a shy judgment on an architect or a contemporaneous building slyly slide into a newspaper or a journal." "No existe la crítica arquitectónica en nuestro país. Se escribe y discute sobre pintura y escultura modernas; poquísimas veces se desliza solapadamente en un periódico, en una revista, algún juicio tímido sobre un arquitecto o un edificio contemporáneos" ("Mientras labran los sillares," *Arquitectura,* 1918: 34; translation here and throughout is by the editors of *Future Anterior*).

[5] Published in *Arquitectura* (June 1918): 31.

[6] "What El Escorial Represents in Our Architectural History," *Arquitectura* 5 (1923): 215.

[7] A good synthesis of this debate in P. Navascués, *Arquitectura española (1808–1914)* (Madrid: Espasa Calpe, 2000), 367–98.

[8] Most significantly *Historia de la arquitectura cristiana española en la Edad Media* (1908) and *Arquitectura civil española de los siglos I al XVIII* (1922). On Lámperez, see P. Moleón, "Vicente Lampérez y el estudio de la arquitectura en la historia," an introductory study in the edition of the first cited work (Madrid: Giner Ediciones, 1993).

[9] Leopoldo Torres Balbás, *Legislación, inventario gráfico y organización de los Monumentos históricos y artísticos de España* (Zaragaoza, Tip. La Editorial, 1919), 21. The text was republished in full recently in *Cuadernos de Arte de la Universidad de Granada* 20 (1989): 195–210.

[10] "La restauration des monuments dans l'Espagne d'aujourd'hui," *Mouseion* 17–18 (1932); and "La reparación de los monumentos antiguos en España," *Arquitectura* 15 (1933): 1.

[11] "El aislamiento de nuestras catedrales," *Arquitectura* 2 (1919): 358.

[12] Published in *Arquitectura* 5 (1923): 305–18. A modern edition was published by the School of Architecture of Granada, 1997.

[13] "La reparación de los monumentos antiguos en España," 1.

[14] *Arte almohade, arte nazarí, arte mudéjar* (Madrid: Plus Ultra, 1949) and *Arquitectura gótica* (Madrid: Plus Ultra, 1952).

[15] Leopoldo Torres Balbás, *Ciudades hispanosumulmanas,* advertencia preliminar, introduction, and conclusion by Henri Terrasse (Madrid: Ministerio de Asuntos Exteriores, Instituto Hispanoárabe de Cultura, 1970).

[16] See J. Calatrava, "El Manifiesto de la Alhambra," in *Estudios sobre historiografía de la arquitectura,* 259–70 (Granada: Editorial Universidad de Granada, 2005).

1. *La Flamme de la Liberté*, Paris (donated by *The International Herald Tribune* to the French people in 1987 and inaugurated in 1989). Exact replica of the flame held by the *Statue of Liberty*, New York (*Liberty Enlightening the World*, 1884–1886) by Frédéric Bartholdi (1834–1904). Due to its proximity to the Alma Tunnel (not accessible to pedestrians) where Lady Diana died in a car accident on August 31, 1997, the monument has been since then reinterpreted by Lady Diana's fans as a cenotaph to her memory. Photograph by the author.

Mario Carpo

The Postmodern Cult of Monuments

Since the first dominion of men was asserted over the ocean, three thrones, of mark beyond all others, have been set upon its sands: the thrones of Tyre, Venice, and England. Of the First of these great powers only the memory remains; of the Second, the ruin; the Third, which inherits their greatness, if it forget their example, may be led through prouder eminence to less pitied destruction.

[Venice] is still left for our beholding in the final period of her decline: a ghost upon the sands of the sea, so weak—so quiet,—so bereft of all but her loveliness, that we might well doubt, as we watched her faint reflection in the mirage of the lagoon, which was the City, and which the Shadow.

I would endeavour to trace the lines of this image before it be for ever lost, and to record, as far as I may, the warning which seems to me to be uttered by every one of the fast-gaining waves, that beat, like passing bells, against the Stones of Venice.

John Ruskin

The resounding opening of John Ruskin's *Stones of Venice* (1851–53)[1] epitomizes the nineteenth-century notion of what monuments are and what they should do. Ruskin turned a whole city into a monument: literally, a warning, an example, and a beacon meant to instruct and inspire, to change the course of history and to guide us toward a better destiny. The same evocative power of objects, and of built and natural landscapes, and their capacity to conjure up meaningful historical narratives form the basis for Ruskin's equally famous "Lamp of Memory" (1849),[2] and would be systematized half a century later by Alois Riegl's seminal taxonomy of monuments, *Der moderne Denkmalkultus*.[3] Riegl's categories held sway throughout most of the twentieth century, and it appears that they often still do, albeit at times unknowingly and uncritically.

Interest in Riegl's theories has risen with the recent revival of architectural interest in monuments, which in turn is part of the vast process of reassessment and reevaluation of iconicity and symbolism in architectural design that started with architectural Postmodernism thirty years ago. Architectural Postmodernism[4] posited that architectural signs may refer to meanings outside architecture proper, either through visual

Future Anterior
Volume IV, Number 2
Winter 2007

similarity (iconicity) or cultural associations (symbolism). This is what most Western monuments with a commemorative value were traditionally meant to do, hence it stands to reason that architectural monuments, which suffered under the rule of modernist ethics, sobriety, and iconoclasm, should thrive again under the influence of postmodernist thought.[5] Architectural Postmodernism is one of the ideological sources of the current renewal of memorial architecture, and this pertains both to new architectural signs designed as monuments, as well as to the memorialization of preexisting objects. Indeed, there is a certain logic in that the ongoing reverse engineering of twentieth-century modernity should bring us back to an auroral state of modernity, namely, to Ruskin's and Riegl's Romantic, and late-Romantic, theories of history. Yet, independent from the ideological content of contemporary memorial programs, it is the architectural materialization of such programs and their specific use of objects, buildings, and places for memorial purposes that may be today partially flawed, and ineffective at best, on account of some crucial changes that have transformed our cultural and technical environment.

Monuments deal with notions and representations of history and time, and their present programs and functions are challenged by changes that have occurred in contemporary philosophy of history and, perhaps more drastically, by the recent ideological perception of a decline (or "end") of history itself. Postmodernism did not mean the same in philosophy as in architectural theory when the term came into currency in the late 1970s.[6] This variance may have led to two very different and possibly opposite views of architectural monuments and of their functions. Jean-François Lyotard's *Postmodern Condition,* published only a couple of years after Charles Jencks's *Post-Modern Architecture,*[7] which architects still tend to know better, was mostly about what we now call "the fragmentation of master narratives," including first and foremost history—in Baudrillard's words, "our lost referential."[8] The decay of all centralized systems (ideological, social, and technological) was central to the critique of what was then called the postindustrial society,[9] and after the fall of the Berlin Wall the postmodernists' end of history[10] was famously reinterpreted by Francis Fukuyama as the end of ideologies, and the end of the most pervasive of all modern ideologies, Hegel's philosophy of history.[11]

Historicism was the framework within which Ruskin's and Riegl's notions of monuments came to light and thrived and indeed a precondition for their very existence. Riegl's definitions of "historical" and "ancient" monuments posit a belief in directional (or teleological) history and presuppose an oriented line of progress (and in the case of Ruskin, an organic simile of rise and decline) within which the modern subject can assess its relative position, take stock of the past, and get ready for the next great leap forward. This once-transparent topography of time may have been lost to postmodern consciousness, but if so, we should also admit that, as a side effect, historical monuments may have been stripped of one of their primary functions. New monuments can have no power of historical orientation because the postmodern vision of history no longer provides any preset line of progress along which historical signs may clearly be situated: as in Fukuyama's Hegelian metaphor of the train, of which some wagons arrive sooner and some later but all on the same track and toward the same destination,[12] it may well be that, as postmodern rails multiply indefinitely, there may be fewer travelers waiting at any station at any given time—or even no travelers at all.

The Eiffel Tower was built—among many other aims—to celebrate technological progress, and as a monument to the seventy-two engineers, scientists, and inventors whose names are inscribed on its metal arches: thinkers whose work, directly or indirectly, made possible the construction of the tower and an iconic indication of more to come following their example and furthering their research. The only twentieth-century monument in Paris that can compare with the Eiffel Tower's popular appeal is, within walking distance of the Tower itself, the so-called memorial to Lady Diana's fatal car accident (a monument that in fact preexisted the event and was recycled as a monument to Lady Diana in the aftermath of the accident).[13] This comparison may suggest that between the times of Gustave Eiffel and those of Lady Diana the ideological and cultural fields where the monument's semantic functions resided may have shifted and that the new field may be objectively reduced in scope and social import. Architectural monuments, which were a vital component of European intellectual life at the end of the nineteenth century, are only marginal cultural players at the end of the twentieth; in true postmodern fashion, their power of incitement to action, insofar as any of it may still exist, seems now reduced to the ambit of micronarratives, microhistories, and microcultures.

To cite another example that likewise highlights the fading social perception of progress, particularly in its most easily quantifiable testimony, technological advancement: the Alpine valleys leading to the Fréjus, or Cenis Rail Tunnel, as well as many neighboring towns and villages in Piedmont and Savoy, are sprinkled with monuments to Germain Sommeiller, the heroic engineer who designed the tunnel and inaugurated it in 1870. The global consequences of computer connectivity at the end of the twentieth century are probably comparable with those that Alpine tunnels had at the end of the nineteenth; yet it is not known that any brick-and-mortar monument may have been dedicated to the inventor of the Internet, whoever he or she may be.

Contrary to their *raison d'être* in the nineteenth century, monuments today seem to be unwilling to provide historical role models, and this abdication of responsibility is in fact already inherent in most of the current memorial practices: contemporary monuments have long stopped celebrating great deeds, as their specialty is to register grave errors; they do not exalt achievement but deplore abomination; and — at least, in nonsocialist countries — it seems we can hardly honor any act of valor accomplished after the end of World War II: the heroes we now tend to remember are most often the inno-cent victims of someone else's crimes. Most of today's monu-ments seem to be reduced to the basic, primeval, and, as Riegl asserted, timeless function of the most ancient of all "intentional" monuments: to mark the graves of the dead, or to remember their burial. Monuments can no longer point to the future because the postmodern construction of history does not provide one, or it provides too many. Historical monuments have no place in posthistorical times.

Parallel and related to cultural irrelevance, monuments conceived in the Romantic tradition now equally face the risk of technological obsolescence and inadequacy. The Romantic definition of monuments as totemic catalysts and activators of memory expected and prompted the simultaneous pres-ence of the monument and of the admonished (one, or more often many) in the same public place. The performative ritual of the act of remembering posited first, the need to go some-where, and then the direct physical experience, optic or tac-tile, of the original monument. Remembrance was predicated upon, and activated by, the experience of a special place or object, often remote or unique, and the view, or vision, of something special. Not coincidentally, the rise of this quest for "experiential travel" is coeval with the development of mass transportation in the nineteenth century. Pilgrims, and grand-tourists, were in the process of becoming mass tourists. Of course mass transportation is still a paradigm of modern life, and even of postmodern life, for that matter. Yet this par-adigm of the mechanical age is increasingly countered by another conflicting paradigm that was started by electricity, then amplified by electronics over the course of the nine-teenth and twentieth centuries.

Electronic technologies of transmission, or transference, are already competing with the older mechanical paradigms of transportation in many aspects of life. No need to go there if the original, or a digital reproduction of it, may come here.[14] And as copyright lawyers and computer hackers know, the electronic distribution of works of art and of their digital copies is already blurring the traditional distinction between originals and reproductions: digital technologies are mostly indifferent to Benjamin's auratic requirements. The combined effects of electronic transference (instead of the traditional need for mechanical displacement) and of digital replication (instead of the traditional authority of the original) may toll the knell of many traditional memorial practices and foster the rise of new ones. As in contemporary media art, the transition from the mechanical to the electronic paradigm has already spawned several generations of hybrids: digital technologies have been merged with or included in traditional memorial programs, ostensibly to complement them or to extend their outreach. But the odd outcomes of these new tools for digitally enhanced mourning also emphasize the rift between old and new memorial practices and cultural technologies.[15] The new information technologies will inevitably remove some deeply rooted memorial traditions from physical space: they will de-spatialize some material repositories of memories, as well as the acts of remembrance that such repositories were meant to ignite. The memorial practices that will decline are those that used to require physical presence in unique, particular, or special places. Those that are on the rise are supported by electronic media and depend on stimuli that are by definition transmissible and replicable. This pattern suggests that monuments in stone may be destined to play a lesser role in the future than they have in the past. They will most likely be replaced by music, voices, words, and all that can be digitally recorded, transmitted, and reenacted. In fact, to some extent this is already happening.[16]

Of course, in spite of significant cultural and technical reasons why monuments may no longer function today as they did a century ago, when their influence and role may have climaxed, the irrational fascination with the magical power of some places—including their power to activate memories—has a long and dignified tradition in the West, and there is no reason this belief should not persist in some form. The Romans called it "genius loci"; the Christians inherited it; the Reformation fought against it, as it deemed this belief a superstition, a relic of paganism, and a possible source of idolatry; the Counter-Reformation defended it, within some limits. Modern science and technology are fundamentally averse to this notion, as both presuppose a neutral space— contrary to the Aristotelian tradition of places, or *topoi,* of which some may differ from others. Some twentieth-century thinkers who took an ideological stance against modern science and technology revived this tradition, and architectural phenomenologists have been particularly active in advocating a born-again power of places, which includes their symbolic and memorial functions. Severed from its ideological motivations, this trend contributed to the wider search for memorial functions in Postmodernist architecture and urban design.

At the same time, it is also evident that the Postmodernist renaissance of monuments that we have been witnessing for at least the last twenty years is pervaded by some nagging feelings of discomfort and unease. Again, this pertains to both sides of the matter: to the design of new, "intentional" monuments as well as to the monumentalization of preexisting objects and to the ensuing policies for their preservation — an entirely different subject, which cannot be discussed here. Evidence of the tensions that characterize a phase of transition is already apparent in one of the texts that marked the beginning of the current culture of monuments. In the preface to first volume of the first edition of his seminal *Lieux de Mémoire,* Pierre Nora envisaged a collection of "memory places," in his words, ranging from the most concrete sense of the term to the most abstract intellectual constructions, which included dictionaries, books, songs, and even Général de Gaulle, considered as the "master totem of our memories."[17] But in the conclusion to the last volume of the series, eight years later, the same author complains that the popular success of his formula, "memory places," has been built upon a fundamental misunderstanding and belies a notion of which "the heuristic interest resided in the dematerialization of 'places,' intended as symbolic instruments."[18] In fact, Nora's memory places were conceived as places within our minds, as in the classical and Renaissance art of memory; instead, they became universally confused with topographical places that generate memories; or, simply, as monuments in the Romantic tradition. They became victims of the Postmodernist cult of brick-and-mortar monuments.

Another symptom of the same uneasiness may be the resistance to the very use of the term *monument,* which in French, for example, has been replaced in most cases by the almost synonymous "*mémorial,*" without any perceivable semantic shift.[19] Some fifteen years ago another ersatz was also tentatively introduced, *historial,* apparently a conflation of *historique* and *mémorial* — a neologism that apparently failed to catch on.[20] A similar shift from *monument* to *memorial* happened in English — witness the title of the very same conference session where an early version of this paper was presented.[21] The polemics concerning the German name of Peter Eisenman's Holocaust Memorial in Berlin — now officially called, solomonically, both *Denkmal* and *Mahnmal*—attest to the onomasiological discomfort generated by the reuse of such ideologically loaded terms as *monument* (in English) and, in German, *Denkmal,* the very term Riegl used in 1903.[22]

Additionally, it is noteworthy that, in spite of the prominent Postmodernist revival of premodern architectural monuments, a strong modernist tradition of antimonumental "living memorials" still carries on relatively unabated. In 1938 Lewis Mumford famously claimed, "if [this] is a monument it is not modern, and if it is modern, it cannot be a monument."[23] This statement is often quoted out of context: its original meaning was more specific than it appears, as Mumford was discussing only funerary monuments and the related cult of death; his stance against monumental burials was part of his sermon on the modern "necropolis" and the antiorganic bias of the mechanical civilization at large. Mumford did admit, however, that he saw no evil in the dedication of some public facility ("a hospital or a power station or an air beacon") as a memorial to a person or an event ("what will make the hospital . . . a good memorial is that it has been well designed for the succor of those that are ill . . . , not the fact that it has taken form out of a metaphysical belief in the fixity and immortality and positive celebration of death").[24] Today, airports are the hottest commodity in the memorial facility business, followed by museums and libraries: hospitals seem to have dropped out of favor.

Evidently, the often ephemeral coupling of a person's name with a public building can do little additional harm to the building itself, regardless of the controversies surrounding the person or the building, taken individually. On the contrary, the indirect (and often uncredited) revival of Riegl's Romantic historicism, and of the Romantic notion of monuments, may have more harmful consequences. Hopefully, these useless new monuments will be simply destined to invisibility—in Mumford's own words, "heaps of stones . . . in the busy streets of our cities, completely irrelevant to our beliefs and demands."[25] For, should such monuments indeed come to function again, then we should come to the conclusion that the memorial programs for which they stood, which were dominant in Europe at the dawn of the twentieth century, may have also been revived, and their content may be reenacted. Given the current frenzy of nationalistic discourse in Europe, the orgy of national anthems, flags, and military pageants sweeping the capitals of the old continent, and the political programs based on the quest for racial and national identities that are being openly discussed in many European Parliaments, this is not an impossible development.

Author Biography

Mario Carpo is an architectural historian and critic and associate professor at the School of Architecture of Paris-La Villette (Paris). He has held teaching and research positions in Europe, the United States, and Canada. His research and publications focus on the relationship between architectural theory, cultural history, and the history of media and information technology. His publications include the award-winning *Architecture in the Age of Printing* (2001), several monographs on Renaissance architectural theory, and essays and articles on contemporary matters published in European and American architectural journals.

Endnotes

An earlier version of this essay was presented at the session "Memorials No More: Desecration, Destruction, Iconoclasm, Neglect," chaired by Andrew M. Shanken at the sixtieth annual meeting of the Society of Architectural Historians, in Pittsburgh, Penn., April 13, 2007. I am thankful to Andrew Shanken and to Jorge Otero-Pailos for their helpful feedback and advice, and to Megan Spriggs for comments, suggestions, and editorial help.

[1] John Ruskin, *The Stones of Venice,* vol. 1, *The Foundations* (London: Smith, Elder and Co., and New York: J. Wiley, 1851), 1–2.

[2] Ruskin, *The Seven Lamps of Architecture* (London: Smith, Elder and Co., 1849), chapter 6.

[3] Aloïs Riegl, K.-k. Zentral-Kommission für Kunst- und historische Denkmale, *Der moderne Denkmalkultus. Sein Wesen und seine Entstehung* (Vienna [etc.]: Braumüller, [1900–] 1903). Available in English as "The Modern Cult of Monuments: Its Character and Its Origin," trans. Kurt W. Forster and Diane Ghirardo, *Oppositions* 25 (Fall 1982): 20–51.

[4] See note 6 below for my reasoning behind the capitalization of *Postmodernism* in this context.

[5] See note 21 below.

[6] A more thorough study of the different original meanings of "postmodernism" in philosophy and in architectural theory falls outside the scope of this brief essay. The two discourses may have been less unrelated than they appear prima facie: the architects' first instantiations of postmodernism in the late 1970s were also based on the demise or rejection of a "master narrative"—the then-dominant discourse of architectural rationalism, predicated on its mandates of technological and social advancement and, in turn, on a historicist teleology of progress and (ultimately) culmination. Likewise, the philosophers' postmodernism (particularly in the Baudrillard declension) had a nostalgic component, particularly with regard to the disappearance of history as the central "referential" then resented as "lost." Regardless, Postmodernist architects famously went on to build or advocate revivalistic, premodern architectural and urban forms, whereas postmodern thinkers often strived to interpret or anticipate a new techno-social and economic environment. This new environment was often seen as evolutionary and in no conflict with the postmodern notions of an "end of history," then more strictly and technically defined as an "end" of Hegelian-based historicism.

This original rift was never healed by subsequent architectural theory and criticism, which came to terms with the vaster philosophical implications of postmodern thinking but could neither hide nor undo what some Postmodernist architects did and still do. Economists and sociologists have long acknowledged that many of the predictions of postmodern philosophers have indeed come true in the 1980s and 1990s, and that some apparently abstract and remote postmodern theories deeply underpin—often unsuspectedly—many aspects of contemporary markets, from financial markets to consumer markets to marketing itself. A similar act of recognition might be beneficial to contemporary media theories, and to architectural theories, as well. In the same way as the economic definitions of "niche markets" and "mass customization" are clear offspring of postmodern theories, it would help to recognize that the current debate on the so-called Web 2.0 is in many ways a debate on postmodernism in disguise, where postmodern categories are put to task to designate a mostly postmodern environment. The same applies to the so-called digital revolution in architecture: from the first definitions of "nonstandard" CAD-CAM to the current debate on versioning, "collective intelligence," and interactive urban technologies, the digital age is most likely, as I argue elsewhere, the real postmodern age of architecture (or architecture turning postmodern in the sense anticipated by postmodern philosophers): the revivalist architectural Postmodernism that started thirty years ago should perhaps be given another name (as in this article it was tentatively differentiated by the use of a capital *P*).

It is sadly ironic, and deeply worrying, that as capitalism is turning post-modern (or Deleuzian, as some say, synecdochically), and architectural and urban design and theories are also turning postmodern in the philosophical sense of the term, at the same time political discourse is oddly becoming Postmodern in the pristine architectural sense of the term — revivalistic, nostalgic, and neo-Romantic (see the conclusion of this article). It is in this context that some contemporary monument building, often prompted by political or ideological programs, may be an ominous sign of worse to come.

[7] Jean-François Lyotard, La condition postmoderne (Paris: Les Éditions de Minuit, 1979); published in English as The Postmodern Condition (Minneapolis: University of Minnesota Press, 1984). Charles A. Jencks, The Language of Post-Modern Architecture (London: Academy Editions, 1977; and New York, Rizzoli, 1977).

[8] Lyotard spoke of the "décomposition des grand Récits," or "métarécits" (La condition Post-Moderne, 31). The "end of history" may have been first proclaimed by Jean Baudrillard, Simulacres et Simulations (Paris: Galilée, 1981), 62–76 (see, in particular, 70: "l'histoire est notre référentiel perdu, c'est-à-dire notre mythe").

[9] On this, see in particular Gilles Deleuze and Félix Guattari, Capitalisme et schizophrénie; 2, Mille Plateaux (Paris: Les Éditions de Minuit, 1980); published in English as A Thousand Plateaus (Minneapolis: University of Minnesota Press, 1987).

[10] Baudrillard eventually refuted the then commonly accepted notion of an "end of history": see in particular his L'illusion de la fin (Paris: Galilée, 1992).

[11] Francis Fukuyama, The End of History and The Last Man (New York: Free Press, 1992). See also Fukuyama, "The End of History?" The National Interest 16 (Summer 1989): 3–18.

[12] Fukuyama, The End of History, 338–39.

[13] See Denise Glück, "Une flamme dans le vent. Un monument pour Lady Diana," in La Confusion des monuments, Cahiers de Médiologie 7, ed. Michel Melot, 229–37 (Paris: Gallimard, 1999).

[14] Paul Valéry famously anticipated a "company for the distribution of sensorial reality to every home," ("Société pour la distribution de la Réalité Sensible à domicile"), similar to the distribution of water and electricity, in an essay of 1929. See his "Conquête de l'ubiquité," in De la musique avant toute chose, 1–5 (Paris: Éditions du Tambourinaire, 1929), 2. Valery's brief text was originally written to advertise a new model of electrical phonograph.

[15] For example, Memory Medallions are digital devices capable of storing text, images, and voice recordings in a medallion that can be affixed to a gravesite or elsewhere, customized and accessible on site and online: Memory Medallion, Inc, "Memory Medallion®. So Future Generations Will Know" (www.memorymedallion.com). Less commercial projects include Cemetery 2.0, "a concept for networked devices that connect burial sites to online memorials for the deceased" (Elliott Malkin, "Cemetery 2.0," www.dziga.com/hyman-victor/) and Michele Gauler, "Digital Remains" (www.michelegauler.net/blog/2006/06/01/digital_remains). See also Eric Krangel, "Coming Soon to a Cemetery Near You: High-tech Tombstones" (jscms.jrn.columbia.edu/cns/2006-12-12/krangel-hightech-tombstones/), and some institutional programs such as the 9/11 Living Memorial, "an online interactive tribute commemorating the lives and stories of September 11" (www.911livingmemorial.org). All Web sites accessed July 14, 2007.

[16] The extension and intensity of the fragments of sensorial experience that can be digitally recorded and transmitted (and in fact recreated, including the possibility of interacting with them) is steadily increasing together with bandwidth and processing power. Already, one may surmise that a wealth of historical video and sound recordings of Général de Gaulle's memorable speeches (available via a variety of public and amateur Web sites) may contribute to the memory of Général de Gaulle's life and achievements more effectively than the ritual pilgrimages to his tomb at Colombey-les-Deux-Églises, where the first stone of a Mémorial Charles-de-Gaulle was laid on the thirty-sixth anniversary of the Général's death on November 9, 2006. The inauguration is planned for 2008: see "Pose de la première pierre du Mémorial Charles-de-Gaulle," www. elysee/fr/elysee/elysee.fr/francais_archives/actualites/deplacements_en_france/2006/novembre/pose_de_lapremier_pierre_du_memorial_charles-de-gaulle.65199.html (accessed July 20, 2007).

[17] Pierre Nora, "Introduction," in Les lieux de mémoire, vol. 1, La République, i–xvi (Paris: Gallimard, 1984), xiii.

[18] Nora, "L'ère de la commémoration," Les lieux de mémoire, vol. 3, Les France, 3, De l'archive à l'emblème, 977–1012, (Paris: Gallimard, 1992); see in particular 1006.

[19] See also Michel Melot, ed., La Confusion des monuments, Cahiers de Médiologie 7 (Paris: Gallimard, 1999).

[20] *Historial de la Grande Guerre,* designed by the architect Henri-Édouard Ciriani, opened to the public on August 1, 1992, as "an international museum of comparative history" on the site of the Battle of the Somme in Picardy: "L"historial de la Grande Guerre," www.historial.org (accessed July 20, 2007).

[21] "Memorials No More." See above.

[22] See Hans-Georg Stavginski, *Das Holocaust-Denkmal: der Streit um das "Denkmal für die ermordeten Juden Europas" in Berlin (1988–1999)* (Paderborn: Schöningh, 2002).

[23] Lewis Mumford, "The Death of the Monument," in *The Culture of Cities,* vii, 6, 433–40 (New York: Harcourt, Brace and Co., 1938), 438. The modernist debate on monumentality (J. L. Sert, F. Léger, S. Giedion, *Nine Points on Monumentality* [1943]; J. L. Sert, *Nine Points for a New Monumentality* [1944]; S. Giedion, *The Need for a New Monumentality* [1944]; etc.) is unrelated to the topic under discussion here. That debate was mostly about the search for a new "monumental" status for modern architecture, based on size, rhetorical effects, and symbolism, which was invoked as a reaction against the antimonumental understatement of the early modernists.

[24] Mumford, "The Death of the Monument," 440.

[25] Ibid.

1. Carlo Scarpa, Museo di Castelvecchio, Verona, Italy, 1956–73. Photograph by author.

Manuel J. Martín-Hernández

Architecture from Architecture
Encounters between Conservation and Restoration

Historians are dedicated to the past, architects to the future. The architectural historian questions the causes that produced an architectural solution. The architect, through the architectural project, ventures an anticipatory creation. Obvious connections between the two tasks are latent: to think about architecture, it is necessary to know its history; to write architectural history can be a way to critique current production. We also know that, in Manfredo Tafuri's words, "as a tool used in the project design, history is sterile."[1] However, there is a direct point of contact between architectural history and architecture, between the past and future: interventions in architectural heritage.

There is no question that architectural heritage needs to be preserved. In this process, preservation becomes a task that keeps the past alive by allowing its entry into the future. Thus, preserving architecture means acknowledging the diverse transformations it has developed over time. Both discourses about the past and future of architecture must coincide to make a successful intervention in cultural heritage.

How do we reconcile these two times? First by spelling out the values that define the heritage in question; then by delimiting the scope of the intervention meant to preserve and invigorate it. Two texts, separated almost by a century, may be of help: the early twentieth-century *Der Moderne Denkmalkultus* (*The Modern Cult of Monuments*) by Alois Riegl, where we find a clear systematization of the values attributed to monuments over time, and the Krakow Charter, the last international document of consensus, approved by the International Conference on Conservation in 2000, which brought together more than three hundred specialists from universities, government offices, and institutions like ICOMOS and ICROMM. Like the 1931 Athens and 1964 Venice Charters before it, this charter attempts to unite the legal resolutions of the member nations in cultural heritage intervention, with a view toward the twenty-first century.[2]

Theorizing Preservation
In Riegl's theory, the most obvious value when referring to cultural heritage is the "age value," which appreciates the past for itself, preventing any intervention from happening. Thus Riegl could say that "the cult of age value brings about its

Future Anterior
Volume IV, Number 2
Winter 2007

own destruction."[3] On the contrary, the "historical value" was inherent in the object's capacity to "represent" a particular time in history, implying that the damaged parts had to be restored so that the object could continue to operate as a "document that must be preserved as intact as possible" for posterity.[4] Riegl resolved the obvious conflict between age value and historic value in favor of the value that the monument had as a document of the past. In this way, "would the monument be about to collapse, no supporter of age value today would oppose preventing the autonomous course of the natural forces."[5] Even more so when the monument was meant by its creators to be maintained "always present and alive," a third value that Riegl called "intentional commemorative." It is precisely this last value that not only leads to the object's conservation but to the interventions destined to revive it.

To these we may add a fourth value, that of "contemporaneity," which may in turn be divided in two: an artistic value and use value. The former was defined by Riegl in his theory of *kunstwollen* (artistic will) as relative, characteristic of each time, and therefore subject to a certain suspension of judgment. The latter referred to the monument's utilitarian capacities, affirming that the only way to safeguard our cultural heritage was to put it to use. It is in this sense that design interventions can be understood.

Such interventions should now overcome the sterile disputes of whether the type of appropriate action must be restoration or conservation—that is the classic nineteenth-century debate that pitted Violet-le-Duc against Ruskin. The Krakow Charter joined conservation and restoration into a single strategy. Its Article 6 states, "conservation requires an appropriate 'restoration project' that defines all the methods and objectives. In many cases, this also requires an appropriate use, compatible with the existing meaning and space."[6] Conservation is enmeshed in intervention. To conserve and design, therefore, are not oppositional activities; on the contrary, both complement each other. Design can learn from conservation's methodology and rigor. Conservation can learn from design that intervention must be understood architecturally according to space, to meaning, to the relation of form to function, and to appropriate techniques. When this mutual instruction happens, historic architecture is allowed to become the protagonist of its own history, in all its complexity. To intervene in cultural heritage is to "re-design" from the standpoint of the architecture itself, acknowledging that such intervention was already present in the architectural object in a "latent form."[7] It follows that the patrimonial quality of architecture will reside, among other things, in its capacity both to resist and adapt itself to the passage of time.

The contemporary emphasis on synthesizing conservation and restoration has implications for architects. This much was already understood by Gustavo Giovannoni (1873–1948), one of the authors of the Athens Charter, who affirmed that the "restoration architect" should fulfill the triple role of "historian, builder, and artist," and also had to "account for the environments' multiple conditions."[8] Giovannoni's theory was truly complex, for it added the need to rehabilitate to the need to conserve. It therefore made every conservation project also a "re-composition" project that had to accommodate new technical methods or new inhabitation conditions into the specific historic environment. Giovannoni placed multiple demands on a single project.[9] These multiple demands, indeed disciplines, had to be reconciled through the architectural project.

Understood as design projects, interventions in architectural heritage cannot obey a priori rules, since each must develop as a response to specific conditions. As Ambrogio Annoni (1882–1954) wrote in the late 1920s, "in front of the monument, *it* is the master; and all work of restoration is determined, in every particular case, from *it*" (emphasis added).[10] That "case by case" methodology was also proposed by Ernesto Nathan Rogers (1909–69), Annoni's successor as chair at the Politecnico di Milano, as a strategy to overcome the abstract universal methods required by official heritage protection regulations. Instead, Rogers thought that interventions in historic environments required architectural projects "that resolve every situation as a defined case with particular conditioning factors."[11] Rogers was not proposing that architects adopt "an agnostic attitude" that accepted any and all methodologies. Rather, for him it was a question of developing a strategic conservation—in the sense we have previously given conservation as an invigorating activity—mindful of the specifics of each historic building or environment. Rogers thought that "conserving and constructing are moments of a single act of conscience, because one and the other are subject to a same method: conservation does not make sense if it is not understood as updating the past, and construction makes no sense if it is not understood as a continuation of the historical process."[12]

This conception of architectural conservation as an act of "re-composition" gave Modern architects the ability to transcend the limitations of previous historicist techniques. A classic example is the work of Carlo Scarpa at the Castelvecchio Museum in Verona, reconstructed between 1957 and 1973. All the recommendations of the Athens Charter are there: contrast between new and old, absence of ornament in the intervention, differentiation in the added elements (like the double façade formed by the old holes and the new carpentry)

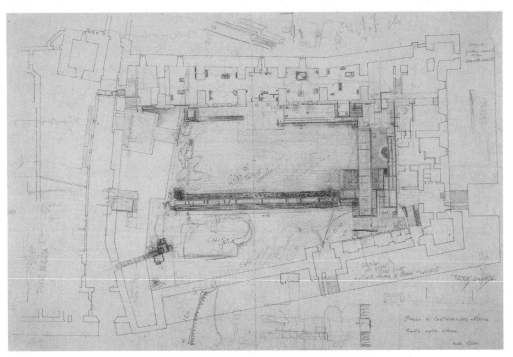

2. Carlo Scarpa and Angelo Rudella, ground-floor plan with final proposal for the garden, 1962–64, n. inv. 31610r—Museo di Castelvecchio, Verona, Italy. Courtesy of the Museo di Castelvecchio, Verona.

and in the materials used (such as the copper roofing to replace missing tiles or the slight separation of the new cement floor from the old walls). Scarpa's understanding of the relationship between conservation and design is evident in his drawings. Significantly, his conceptual montages presented the original medieval building alongside references of contemporary architecture.[13] The drawings that he produced in developing his design employed various techniques to represent the accumulation of time, something he felt gave character and vitality to historical buildings. He traced over lines and watercolored or sketched repeatedly over the same cardboard. He also superimposed transparencies of all the floors and ceilings to develop the new structural mesh as an integral part of original building, a method he also employed to situate each artwork precisely.

Intervention as Preservation

The "environmental" principles of Giovannoni were incorporated in the 1931 Athens Charter and applied to historic urban centers in the 1964 Venice Charter.[14] His environmental thesis has not been well understood by those who believe the old and the new to be incompatible, out of a close-minded conception of historic values. Today, in countries like Spain, Italy, or Greece, the specific laws of protection have frozen the architecture of many historical urban centers in pure façadism, causing them to lose vitality and functionality. This is what Cesare Brandi defined as a crime of "falsification,"[15] a process in which cultural norms force interventions to "cover up" with

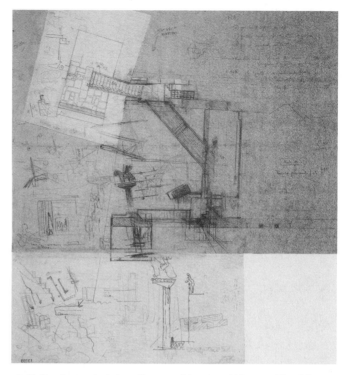

stylistic elements taken from architectural history. The false operates perniciously in contemporary society, as Guy Debord noted in his *Comments on the Society of the Spectacle:* "What is false creates taste, and reinforces itself by knowingly eliminating any possible reference to the authentic."[16] The failure to understand architectural design as an integral part of conservation has often led to the reduction of historic architecture to a mere stage set for the contemporary architectural drama unfolding in front of it.

Fortunately, the Krakow Charter aims to end these practices. In defining the city as an "organic unity" (Article 8), only the maintenance of certain dimensions or certain spatial and chromatic characteristics are required but not stylistic similarity with forms of the past. Defending the contemporary interventions as integral parts of the restoration of monuments, Article 4 states: "The reconstruction of entire parts 'in the style of the building' should be avoided.... If necessary, for a proper use of the building, completion of more extensive spatial and functional parts should reflect contemporary architecture." This principle is transferable to interventions on an urban scale, so that plans to protect historical environments should take into account urban evolution and be considered more as processes than as finished interventions.

As we can see in Alvaro Siza's Centro Galego de Arte Contemporaneo (Santiago de Compostela, 1988–93), contemporary interventions can safeguard the urban structures that are the real foundation of the historic city without treating

4. Alvaro Siza, Centro Galego de Arte Contemporaneo, Santiago de Compostela (Spain), 1988–93, confronted to Monasterio de Santo Domingo de Bonaval (ss. XIII–XVIII). Photograph by author.

history as a stage set. This is made possible by grasping and expressing the structuring features of the place to be preserved. An architectural intervention need not freeze the historic environment in which it is inserted. It may perform the opposite function: giving new life to the historic city or building.

Author Biography
Manuel J. Martín-Hernández is professor of architectural composition and former dean (1999–2003) at the School of Architecture of the University of Las Palmas de Gran Canaria, Spain. His research covers the theory, criticism, and history of architecture and architectural intervention in the built heritage. He has taught in numerous doctoral and masters programs in European and Latin American universities. His recent publications include *La Invención de la Arquitectura* (1997), *La Tipología en Arquitectura* (2004), and other texts on urbanism, design, and architectural heritage. As a practitioner he has contributed to the inventory of Canarian heritage and executed a number of planning projects in historical centers.

Endnotes
Translated by Carlos Huber Suchowiecky.
A previous version of this article was presented at the Annual Conference of Spanish Art Historians in November of 2006.
[1] Manfredo Tafuri, *Teorías e Historia de la Arquitectura* (Barcelona: Laia, 1972), 282–83. Vittorio Gregotti wrote that history "presents itself as a curious instrument whose knowledge seems indispensable but, once acquired, is not usable directly" (*El Territorio de la Arquitectura* [Barcelona: G. Gili, 1972], 154).
[2] The first was an agreement reached at the conclusion of the Conference of Experts for the Protection and Conservation of the Monuments of Art and of History, convened by the International Office of Museums (League of Nations) and celebrated between October 21 and 30 of 1931. The second was the document approved at the close of the Second International Congress of Architects and Technicians of Historic Monuments (UNESCO) held between May 25 and 31 of 1964.
[3] Alois Riegl, *El Culto Moderno a Los Monumentos. Carácter y Origen,* (1903; Madrid: Visor, 1987), 54.
[4] Ibid., 58. Riegl even proposed the substitution of parts of monuments for better copies. This now happens with many archaeological and sculptural pieces.
[5] Ibid., 62–63.
[6] The text of the Krakow Charter is available at www.ruraleurope.org/pdf/ KRAKOW.pdf.

[7] Paolo Torsello, *Restauro architettonico* (Milan: F. Angelli, 1989), 68.

[8] Gustavo Giovannoni, "I restauri dei monumenti e il recente congresso storico" (1903), in *Dal Capitello alla Città*, ed. G. Zucconi, 97–102 (Milan: Jaca Book, 1996), 100.

[9] "Architects are often missing culture, historical criteria, and humanistic preparation; art historians are not educated in the reasons and technical methods that constitute and determine the foundation of architectural composition." My translation from Gustavo Giovannoni, "La architettura italiana nella storia e nella vita" (1920), in *Dal Capitello alla Città*, ed. G. Zucconi, 74–78 (Milan: Jaca Book, 1996), 75.

[10] Ambrogio Annoni, "Criteri e saggi per la conservazione e il restauro degli antichi edifici nel moderno rinovamento delle città" (1929), in *Scienza ed Arte del Restauro Architettonico*, 73–77 (Milan: Artistiche Framar, 1946), 76. Annoni was a disciple of Camillo Boito (1836–1914), the founder of the Italian School of Restoration and advocate of the so-called scientific restoration and of the precise distinction between existing parts and new interventions.

[11] Ernesto N. Rogers, "Verifica culturale dell'azione urbanística" (1958), in *Esperienza dell'architettura*, 291–93 (Milan: Skira, 1997), 292.

[12] Ibid.

[13] See Ignasi Solà-Morales, "Dal contrasto all'analogia," *Lotus* 46, (1985): 40–42. Also see Licisco Magagnato, "Storia e genesi dell'intervento del museo di Castelvecchio," *Quaderns* 158 (1983): 25–40. It is important not to forget that Scarpa worked in constant dialogue with Licisco Magagnato, the museum director.

[14] For example, in Article 6: "When a traditional environment remains, it shall be preserved; on the contrary, any new construction, destruction, or use that might alter the relationship between the volumes and colors must be rejected." And in Article 7: "The monument cannot be separated . . . from the environment in which it is found."

[15] "Falsification" would be the production of an object in the likeness of the ways or style of a particular historical period with the objective to "deceive" with regards to the period, material, technique, or author of the object. See "Falsificazione," appendix to Cesare Brandi, *Teoria del restauro* (Turin: Einaudi, 1977), 66.

[16] Guy Debord, *Comments on the Society of the Spectacle*, trans. Malcolm Imrie (London: Verso, 1990), 50.

1. Lopud's Franciscan monastery viewed from the bay. Photograph by Jorge Otero-Pailos.

2. Exterior view of Your Black Horizon T-B A21 pavilion by architect David Adjaye and artist Olafur Eliasson, as sited in Lopud's olive groves, close to the Franciscan monastery. Photograph by Todd Ebberle.

Preservation, Contemporary Art, and Architecture

Thyssen-Bornemisza Art Contemporary (T-B A21), under the leadership of Francesca von Habsburg, convened experts from the worlds of preservation, art, and architecture to a series of intimate roundtables, which took place on the island of Lopud, Croatia, between June 18 and 20, 2007, as part of the symposium "Patronage of Space." More information on the symposium can be found at www.tba21.org. The following is an edited and abbreviated transcript of the June 18 roundtable "Preservation and Reanimation through Contemporary Art and Architecture," which included Andreas Ruby (moderator), Francesca von Habsburg, Albert Heta, Jorge Otero-Pailos, Dinko Peračić, François Roche, and Mark Wigley.

FRANCESCA VON HABSBURG: Andreas Ruby recently told me that many things have ended in Dubrovnik, for one reason or another. I thought that we should focus the next couple of days on initiating things in Dubrovnik instead! I truly appreciate the interdisciplinary nature of this panel.

This morning, we all visited the Franciscan monastery. For about five years, I've been trying to reconcile its adaptive reuse for both private and public purposes with a sensitive restoration guided by principles of maximum retention of original substance. We've had a number of different opinions, discussions, and arguments about how this monastery should be restored. Having been actively involved in heritage preservation since the early 1990s, I naturally realize how complex and demanding the practice of conservation is. When you are restoring something, the first question that you ask is, how you are going to use it? My vision of the monastery's future combines a home with a retreat for scholars to be creative and develop ideas, it includes use of some of the larger spaces for contemporary art interventions and projects, possibly mini-exhibitions, particularly performances in the large fortress in the back. The complex is actually a fortified monastery, which included a pharmacy, with a treatment center, and most likely a medicinal garden. It has a religious history as well as a protective function, along with the historical role that the Franciscan order had in the education of the community. I see here a link to the process of restoring the historical Renaissance gardens of Lopud and creating a special botanical garden there, as another logical part of the revitalization of the island. The

Future Anterior
Volume IV, Number 2
Winter 2007

historical importance of botany and medicinal plants of Renaissance Dalmatia is directly connected to the Franciscan
order, which was very committed to these remedies and
their pharmacies from the thirteenth century onward.

You have also visited Olafur Eliasson and David Adjaye's
beautiful, extraordinary art pavilion, a contemporary art and
architecture collaboration that T-B A21 commissioned two
years ago and that was first shown at the 51st Venice Biennial
in 2005, and is now rebuilt a stone's throw from the monastery.

I'd like to start this debate by asking Jorge to talk about
his impressions, because he's got a very interesting study group
at Columbia University, which I believe is extremely relevant
to this discussion.

JORGE OTERO-PAILOS: We're in a historical moment in which art
and architecture are beginning to rediscover each other through
historic preservation. In order to make valuable discoveries in
each other, these three disciplines must lower their guards.
The question for me is how can we lower the guard of preservation, which is so much about guarding — protecting heritage — so that it becomes open to other interpretations of
heritage that are not intradisciplinary but that are extra-
disciplinary and that come from art and architecture. I think
that is where the contribution of the pavilions, already seen
as part of Lopud's heritage, is really quite striking. The pavilion allows us to ask questions of this historic site that might
not have been possible within just the realm of conservation.
How can historic Lopud inform contemporary art and aesthetic perception? Questions like this are not considered
legitimate in historic preservation. So the mere fact that you
are beginning to open up a space for asking questions that
are in a sense guarded or forbidden, so to speak, in preservation is a huge contribution. I hope that in the process of
our discussions, we will begin to make those discoveries of
things that were unanticipated somehow, of new methods
and ways of thinking about heritage that have been excluded from the heritage discussion in order to really further
a way of thinking about heritage. Today, connections are
more important than boundaries, and preservation is all
about setting boundaries, setting boundaries about what
you can touch and what you cannot touch, what is excluded
and what is included, where history begins and where it
ends. We legislate what is a monument and what, two
meters away from it, is not. We are beginning to question
those boundaries here. I'm very excited to be here and be
a part of this, and I'm looking forward to lowering my guard
and seeing what other people can contribute and bring into
the discussion of preservation.

3. Video still of the debate. At the table, from right to left: Albert Heta, Jorge Otero-Pailos, Francesca von Habsburg, Andreas Ruby, Dinko Peračić, François Roche, and Mark Wigley (obscured by audience). Courtesy T-B A21, Vienna.

ANDREAS RUBY: Maybe you could think about what comes after the guarding paradigm. It wouldn't exactly be the total opposite of it, like just letting go, but something in between. It's clear that it's a highly political situation. On the one hand, you have this extreme petrifaction of the past in the name of authenticity, and on the other hand, you have situations where the past is just bulldozed as if nothing had happened since the tabula rasa days of modernism, like in China where old villages or old city cores are replaced by big high rises and CBDs. I think there must be a way to negotiate the past and the present, and that transition would be interesting to think about. Is there a way to acknowledge the past but not enslave yourself to it? Is there a way to tie the future into the past without annihilating the past? This type of continuity seems to have no lobby yet. The preservationists seem to be the lobbyists of the guarding paradigm. Then you have the post-, post-, post-transmodernists who still believe in inventing an entirely new future, as we can see in the tiger states of Asia where the past simply has no lobby. It could be interesting to think about that almost seamless transition between past, present, and future. It seems that there existed a knowledge of this transition, if we look back in history when, for instance, Christian monasteries were built in the remainders of old Roman baths that were destroyed in the big migration wars in the fifth and sixth and seventh centuries. There was no idea of rebuilding them but rather using them as a raw construction, infrastructure—sheer matter, in fact—tied into the hardware of another structure yet to come, with often totally contradicting ideological premises. I mean, there couldn't be a bigger gap than between the hedonist space of a Roman bath and a Christian monastery for men only. Unless you think that there's an anticipation of a gay club. That type of sovereignty, of dealing with history by incorporating its material traces while giving them a new programmatic trajectory, is something that we can find in different periods of history but is somewhat lacking today. And I'm wondering why that is so and whether we can find again that kind of spirit.

FRANCESCA VON HABSBURG: Albert, you have a problem rising in Priština now, which revolves around the reconstruction of an old *hammam*. Please tell us about it.

ALBERT HETA: First of all, I don't come from a background of architecture, I'm an artist, and I'm a bit more critical toward an approach that is currently being used in the countries of this region. Here, basically, heritage is politics, politics is memory, and heritage is used to either erase a part of our memory or to create a forceful image that didn't exist before. Together with some colleagues, we are working on a project called Architecture of Freedom, which investigates what happens in a country after liberation or after an emergency situation. It is like trying to follow these bits and pieces of history in creation — of a forceful, nonexistent history in creation. A part of the story is an old Turkish bath, a *hammam,* in Priština that was built in the fifteenth century, during the Ottoman Empire, and today the local government is trying to restore it and possibly turn it into a European cultural center. For me this approach, or similar ones, look like acts of total colonization, like the cultural colonization of a space that used to function as a router for the citizens of Priština, as a gathering space, as a relaxing place during times of peace. Today, this already dead building is being restored and made dead again, because it is being isolated from the people and not allowed to communicate with the people where it is located. Similar initiatives exist in the region. The most extreme case in Kosovo is the issue of cultural heritage, which, in the process of political negotiations, had the biggest importance, or at least the biggest space. A large amount of "Serb" Orthodox churches are in Kosovo right now, and that cultural heritage today is politicized because it is ethnicized. The churches don't belong to the people. They belong only to an ethnicity, and through those churches one part of the population is claiming a territory. The churches have been awarded a certain amount of land around them. If there were more churches they would have more land. It is as if, if you had eight monasteries, then you could claim independence. In this case, through five or six churches they will have under control 28 percent of the territory of the country. So heritage in Kosovo is only political; it doesn't belong to experts or to culture per se. It is an issue that is highly politicized. We are starting a debate to tackle a few issues and to basically throw a "virus" in that environment, a critical virus, and we aim to address these issues on another level that doesn't exist right now down there.

4. Restoration work in Lopud's fortress. The site where a new recording studio and media center for T-B A21's upcoming commissions and performance projects will find place. The change in color of the stone wall marks the depth of the recent excavation. Photograph by Jorge Otero-Pailos.

Jorge Otero-Pailos: I think that's an important point to bring in, to remind preservation of politics, because so often preservation stands back and assumes the mantle of detachment of the architectural historian or the art historian. But in fact, when you look at the history of preservation, it is intimately linked with war. Not just here but also in the United States, where the early stirrings of a preservation consciousness began with the 1863 Lieber Code, which established the rules of engagement during the Civil War and regulated what could be done to captured enemy property. It addressed a fundamental preservation question by asking, when we fight each other, what are we going to retain from each other's heritage? The Lieber Code also served as the basis for the 1929 Geneva Convention. Today we are beginning to look on the destruction of heritage as a war crime. French preservation also had its origins in civil war, the French Revolution. When revolutionaries went about destroying all signs of the monarchy, intellectuals stepped back and said, "We must de-politicize architecture. These are beautiful buildings, forget about their political symbolism and let's just preserve them for their aesthetic and stylistic value." That was the beginning of preservation's invocation of style as a means to depoliticize architecture. The interesting part of the conversation with the conservators of the monastery was that they can't seem to find the style for it. This absence of a style creates a crisis within preservation because, then, on what grounds do you preserve it? The question of politics immediately follows, but we haven't gotten to that yet . . .

FRANÇOIS ROCHE: It's very strange how our future is a sensation of the past, it's nostalgia. Our future has been designed in the sixties and there is a vintage sensation of the future. So I don't know how we could introduce preservation in this world; it is very difficult for me to use. There is an hour of time between past and future, hesitating, palpitating between both sensations. It is something very interesting, in a way. I remember a movie of Kiyoshi Kurosawa, *Charisma,* about a tree, a very old tree, which illustrates the social pressures historic preservation faces. In the movie the tree was at first protected because it was the oldest in the forest. But the community found out that the tree was infiltrating the ground and toxifying the real forest, which was the source of the local economy. So they decided to destroy the tree, because it was not preserving what the humans created after the dinosaur period. So do we need to preserve the toxicity of the monastery or do we need to inject a new toxicity into the monastery?

ANDREAS RUBY: Couldn't we also understand historic preservation as that which is less value laden, something like a transformation, which may have a whole variety of connotations but which does not imply that any one period has any kind of moral sovereignty over any other. If we take this monastery as an example, there is an interest in keeping it as historical heritage, but there is also a need to reprogram it. Francesca, what is the challenge for you, the monastery's history or the potential that you can see connected to it?

FRANCESCA VON HABSBURG: I walked into that building ten years ago. It was a really terrible ruin with most of its roof missing. However, I felt the stones were alive and there was still an incredible vivacity to the place. It had been abandoned about one hundred fifty years ago, and many people had used, abused, and looted it since then. When the Italian fascists came here in the Second World War they wrote "Il Duce" in big graffiti on a wall, adding yet another incredible layer to the site's history. What I want to preserve is the memory of the monument with all its different layers, also including part of the condition that it's in now. This concept is very difficult to get through to the Institute of Protection of Monuments because for them it's crucial to restore the original condition as best as possible, obviously erasing records of recent neglect.

In view of the discrepancy between my intended reuse of the complex and the conservation authorities' insistence on complete restoration, I commissioned Janet Cardiff, a Canadian artist, to create a "video walk" through the monastery. She has already been here twice, filming, documenting, and immersing herself in the multilayered history of the complex, and she will come back for several more visits. The final project will incorporate these many visits into one video walk, drawing the viewer into Janet's imagination. In parts of the walk one will be able to see the process of change—and that's the only way I could recapture that memory. Interestingly, working with a contemporary artist has become the most efficient way to keep this memory alive. I know that once the building is finished, it will be very difficult to recollect those years spent battling with its restoration. It is also my intention to revitalize the fortress and transform it into a creative platform for new artworks. This has now led to other new commissions such as Olafur's project to create a hanging bridge that creates an essential new public access to the fortress from the monastery. Catherine Sullivan will come and create a new work here in the fall based on Shakespeare's *Twelfth Night* and the dual sexual roles of the two main characters that he created for his play, using Illyria as a backdrop. It's really important to me that the walls of the fortress not turn into a stage backdrop but rather become an integral part of the creative process of the artists' projects, thus giving new meaning and purpose (form and function) to the building.

I am very interested in the work of people who have an unusual sensitivity and approach to the context of a site.

ANDREAS RUBY: Dinko, what do you think would have happened to the monastery if Francesca hadn't come along ten years ago and said, "I want to do something with it." What would the normal state of affairs be in Croatia?

DINKO PERAČIĆ: I'd like to extend this conversation a bit to contextualize and to understand what preservation means, in a wider sense, in Croatia. Everyone at the moment knows that Croatia is an undeveloped or untouched country, especially its coastal ports, and because of the global pressure and because of many other influences, it is going to be built up very soon. Croatia is becoming a major tourist destination. In tourism, authenticity is what is sold as the content. The result

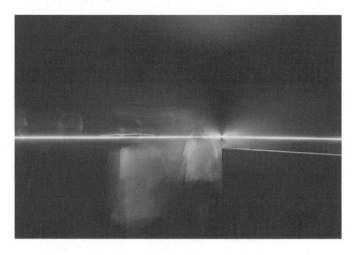

5. The participants of the roundtable inside the Your Black Horizon pavilion. The line of artificial light changes in color to match that of the sky in Lopud. A full day of color variations is compressed into seventeen minutes. Photograph by Todd Ebberle.

is a kind of projection of a wish for authenticity onto our architecture. Everyone wants something that looks old and kind of made in an old way. Authenticity has become our national objective. The marketing slogan for Croatia is "the Mediterranean as It Once Was," and we are also supposed to live in that place as it used to be. And the people are being asked to create this tourist product. All these people are in a way creating this Mediterranean as it once was. Not a Mediterranean as it could be, or as it has to be. In Split, there is a slogan: "Split Is a City Where the Time Stands Still." Try to imagine your own countries' societies as places where time is stopped. What I am really interested in is to find out what could be extrapolated from this story about the history of Croatian architecture. I'm really curious about developing, extrapolating the methods and principles by which we can talk about history as a living system rather than as a style.

JORGE OTERO-PAILOS: I agree that methods are important and should be rethought. Finding similarities in how we do things is a first step toward interdisciplinary work. For instance, the principle of reversibility is central to conservation practice. In other words, if you do something and you do it improperly, somebody in a future generation might be able to do it better. It's very interesting that the only way to get the pavilion built was to pitch it as a kind of reversible intervention. It's considered a temporary pavilion by the buildings department. It's seen as a kind of test. I think that's really the level at which the discussion is operative and very fruitful, in the sense that the very concept that is central to preservation, and that makes preservation the most conservative, so to speak, has now been able to be deployed as the most progressive kind of principle, enabling this radical pavilion to be built in the island of Lopud. It is at that methodological level that I think there is an opportunity to bridge the worlds of art, architec-

6. From right to left: Francesca von Habsburg, Andreas Ruby, and Dinko Peračić. Photograph by Todd Ebberle.

ture, and preservation. How could we develop that? What would it be to think about the coast of Croatia as a kind of reversible coast? What would it be to have a reversible development, as opposed to sustainable development?

FRANCESCA VON HABSBURG: I think that, in a way, I was describing Janet's project in the monastery because I felt that it integrated the creative process into the conservation work, as opposed to commissioning a project for a finished space. Integrating contemporary expression into a historical monument, as opposed to juxtaposing them later, seems far further reaching and innovative. It's a similar process to the one that David and Olafur went through: the building and the artwork were actually created and conceived simultaneously. If I take a few steps back and look at the revitalization of Lopud, as opposed to just restoring the monastery, I see Lopud as an extraordinary, pristine place that really has the potential of being developed far differently than the terrifying way that Dinko just described as the future vision for tourism in Croatia. It could become a cultural hub of contemporary expression, a place of reference and inspiration. The pavilion itself is something that can revitalize only part of the island; I can't imagine it revitalizing the whole island because, obviously, it also depends on the economy generated by conventional tourism to survive. However, parachuting a wonderful project into a beautiful location is simply not enough. We needed to trigger an interaction. The question remains: how does it resonate with the landscape as well as the community? Learning to read the ripple effect it creates as opposed to creating a tidal wave of change is the key. We are really here asking ourselves these questions, how does this work and how could it work in the future, what would be the potential of leaving a pavilion here "full time"? And what effect would it have on the island and what would it generate, if anything at all? It could be possibly easily dismissed, nobody bothering to even come out here to visit it. I do believe in setting up a project that then poses such questions, then waiting for the response before moving forward and planning more projects, because I think it's practically impossible to have clear guidelines on how to revitalize or how to breathe life into something. This remains an experiment for me!

MARK WIGLEY: The two projects, the contemporary art pavilion just constructed and the restoration of an old building as an ongoing long project, are kind of like a textbook, a brilliant textbook argument about the nature of art, preservation, and architecture because, so clearly and so strongly—as Jorge made evident earlier—the pavilion is a preservation job. Even from the most simple sense it's a preservation of the pavilion in Venice. Very precise observations, scientific observations, have been made on the differences of the light in the place, the light on the outside but also the light on the actual horizon line itself. On the other hand it's very clear that the restoration job on the monastery is radical art, is a radical transformative act, a revitalizing act of art. It's a radical step, and in neither case should that come as any surprise to us, because in any case preservation is extremely radical. To put it one way, to preserve something is to change it, and so preservationists are people who change things because they don't let them be. The primary purpose of architecture is to reveal change and to reveal it by not changing it, so it's slow. We want the house always just to be sitting there, so the responsibility of the architect is always to go against time, and so the preservationist interestingly enough enters into the situation and in fact invigorates the architecture and puts it into time. Which is why as long as we think of the preservationists as the morticians, preserving the past, versus the artists and architects as the revolutionaries who change the future such that the preservationists have to see the artists as their enemy, we fail to see the more-or-less conservative nature of architects and artists and the more-or-less radical nature of preservationists. The past is always a project. The past is not something that happened, it's a project that you throw into the future, and you choose your weapons to make the throw. The preservationist field is an expert at a certain kind of throw, which will give us in the future a mythical past. It's always mythical. So the question is, what kind of throw, what kind of myth? And in the case of the monastery, there are many different kinds of throws, and the object itself is layered. Preservationists are radical, and they must take responsibility of their radical techniques. Literally, we saw stone walls with hypodermic needles, and no architect ever uses technology as good as that. It's the preservationists that have all the best tricks. But it's done in the name of the past, in the name of no change, but it's all about radical change, and I think the primary focus is to encourage preservationists to see what they are themselves in fact doing and become a little more creative in the moves they make. Survival is based on openness to mutation and then a kind of resolute dogma. And I think what we need to do is to construct a preservation discipline, which is absolutely stubborn — legally and technologically stubborn — and also able to mutate.

ALBERT HETA: I do not think that all your theories can be applied everywhere. Where I come from, heritage, or let's say preservation, is seen as the biggest enemy, right now. The people in that territory would like there to be no particular heritage in that territory — none whatsoever — precisely because historic preservation is used by the former occupiers of the country as a tool for clear political aims. The problem, I think, is when heritage is turned into something ethnic.

MARK WIGLEY: Actually I don't agree, and I want to say that I conceded on all of this. Actually I think it's not true. If those who have political authority over preservation, for example, were operating in a way you are describing, it would be impossible to resist them. In this situation, it's impossible to resist such forces if they are positioned as, let's say, conservative protectionists, guarding versus, let's say, another discourse that is understood to be multiple, open, diverse, and so on. I think the only politically effective act is to sort of publicly and clearly identify the radical nature of that so-called protectionism: in other words, the radical repressions that are involved in constructing that particular heritage image. It's the only way to change it, and as long as the battle is constructed as progressives versus conservatives, it's a disaster, because, actually, the real progressives in that sense are the preservationists who are usually redesigning — as in this case — an entire nation, the aesthetics of an entire nation. And this kind of politics is really politics as a work of art. I agree the language is offensive. The situation is offensive. But it's really happening. It's not only happening here. It's the way things work. It's part of the engineering of tourism, but tourism itself is one of the master industries of forgetting all that was done in the name of memory.

ANDREAS RUBY: Maybe an architect, now, in order to change something, needs to step in and take the role of preservationist. From history we can learn that the true nature of preservation is transformation. If I make a statement or intervention that radically changes the situation, I'm actually making a preservative act. Obviously that challenges the self-understanding of the discipline so far, because, as you said, even if preservation undertakes these radical changes, they always do it for the sake or in the name of keeping things as they are. So the question is, how can you break up the self-image of preservation and how can you change the idea of what a preservationist does?

Fʀᴀɴçᴏɪs Rᴏᴄʜᴇ: In reviving the past, it's important to invent a ceremony and not only a cleansing of the stone. We have to create a social protocol for our ceremony. You talk about Frankenstein, but I'm more interested in Mephisto. Mephisto is a deal with yourself, just as Faust is a deal with yourself. It's not the alien outside yourself as a perfect example of your integrity. It's inside you. The devil, the evil, or the hell is in you. So how can we re-create a palpitating ceremony in reviving? I remember when Pierre Huyghe invented a new ceremony in upstate New York, for a project for the Dia Art Foundation. The whole town needed to gather one day per year—with all the trucks, all the babies, all the cows, all the animals, and all the cats—everybody needed to be on the streets, to perform a ceremony, and to reinvent paganism, to reinvent the fact that the day is a pure ceremonial festive system. So if we want to revive the stone, it's to put Mephisto inside the stone; it's to put earth palpitating, to revive the *mode d'emploi,* to invent operating instructions. Yes, there is a narrative; we introduce a narrative function, which is not only functional/re-functional of the iconography of the existing patrimonial system, but we introduce a narrative way to deal with this dead body coming back from the grave and to say "hello!" So we have to write a scenario for this narrative revival of the dead body—as a ceremony. The ceremony is important. We don't want to re-create a Franciscan monk but a kind of conspiracy. We could imagine a conspiracy: people leaving the tower, something appears, not only the stone, something growing. We don't know exactly what has happened, but finally people become afraid of what is happening and, at the same time, create the desire and give impetus to the rumor. The rumor is incredible, a key to revival—the rumor of this palpitating body after death. What is happening after the death experience, after the tunnel? One should talk about this freaky experience.

Aɴᴅʀᴇᴀs Rᴜʙʏ: But I think it's important that you said the ceremony should not be the same ceremony that it has been. You're saying that the stone is not enough; we need to invent some kind of scenario that helps us to use it as an infrastructure for life and not as a fetish that is of a museum. I think that's probably what you're doing. You're trying to create that type of ceremony that helps us to see in it more than stone.

FRANCESCA VON HABSBURG: There is this need and desire, and, of course, there is a freshness in designing your own building, something new, and it's really difficult to find an architect who's really willing to look at the old building and help you reinterpret it. This is a discussion — how do you do that? Contemporary architects find it very difficult to get excited about these kinds of problems, and conservation architects are bogged down in theory, are very restricted in their ideas.

JORGE OTERO-PAILOS: Preservation is not just working on monuments but also includes these kinds of performance pieces — ceremonies if you will — that happen during the process of visiting historic sites. Preservation organizes how one visits. In fact, I define preservation as the organization of attention. It's the kind of organization of attention that is all about distracting. It's distracting you from looking at that which you are not supposed to be looking at. For instance, think about the coast here and the whole branding of Croatia as "The

Mediterranean as It Used to Be." It's interesting that it's diverting you from Croatia as it used to be. The whole organization of your attention is toward the Mediterranean, and that's the whole journey and the whole experience that you're supposed to have. But what would happen if we were to re-slogan Croatia in the journals and travel magazines as "Croatia as It Used to Be." That alone would reorganize attention.

ALBERT HETA: Croatia during Ante Pavelić! In terms of preservation, it is like asking if the Taliban were doing preservation when they destroyed the Bamiyan Buddhas.

MARK WIGLEY: Yes, from a stupidly abstract point of view, the Taliban have to be understood as expert preservationists. One could look at the Taliban arguments made during the moments of maximum violence, and the language there would be a language of preservation. Of course, it's the preservation of the self and destruction of the other. Not only is preservation always haunted by simultaneous protection and violence, but there's always violence in preservation. One wonders to what extent the sort of Western legitimization of those figures also led to their destruction.

FRANCESCA VON HABSBURG: I heard the bells of the church of the Franciscan monastery ring ten times, and this is actually dinnertime. I think the thought of the reconstruction of the Bamiyan Buddhas as being a horrendous gesture is something we all agree about.

Panelist Biographies
Francesca von Habsburg is the founder of T-B A21, the Thyssen-Bornemisza Art Contemporary Foundation, based in Vienna, Austria. In 1989, after working in London, New York, and Los Angeles, she became chief curator of special exhibitions of the Thyssen-Bornemisza collection at the Villa Favorita in Lugano. In 1995, she founded ARCH Foundation, which is dedicated to the preservation and restoration of cultural heritage.

Albert Heta is an artist and cofounder of Stacion Center for Contemporary Art, Prishtina. His solo exhibitions, public projects, and interventions include "It's Time to Go Visiting: No Visa Required" (2003), a public intervention on British Airways billboards in Prishtina; "Happiness-Independence Day: 1 Minute" (2001), the appropriation of the speech of the UN Administrator of Kosova aired on public television of Kosova in 2001; "Kosovar Pavilion" Venice Biennale 2005, La Biennale di Venezia 51; and "Embassy of the Republic of Kosova," Cetinje, SCG (2004), at the Fifth Biennial of Cetinje.

Jorge Otero-Pailos is founder and editor of *Future Anterior* and assistant professor of historic preservation at Columbia University. His research focuses on the history and theory of modern historic preservation and architecture. He lectures internationally and has published widely in journals such as *JSAH, Postmodern Culture, Journal of Architectural Education, Volume, City, BAU,* and others. He has received numerous research grants and has held postdoctoral fellowships at the Canadian Center for Architecture and the American-Scandinavian Foundation. He is also a practicing architect and serves as vice president of DoCoMoMo US.

Dinko Peračić is an architect and the cofounder of Platforma 9.81, a group for research in architecture and urbanism. He is editor of the interdisciplinary project "Tourist Transformations," which deals with changing conditions of the tourist zones, and also is a partner in ARP, an architecture studio.

François Roche is an architect and partner, with Stéphanie Lavaux, in Roche DSV, a practice based in Paris and La Réunion, which focuses on the bond between building, context, and human relations. With the agency *R&Sie . . .*, Roche and Lavaux are currently undertaking a critical experiment with new warping technologies to prompt architectural "scenarios" of cartographic distortion, substitution, and genetic territorial mutations.

Andreas Ruby is a Berlin-based critic and curator in the fields of architecture, design, and visual arts. He works under the agency Textbild in collaboration with his partner Ilka Ruby. He writes essays and reviews for architectural magazines including *Daidalos* (for which he also served as the executive editor), *Bauwelt, Assemblage, Archis, Architektur Aktuell, Werk,* and *Bauen + Wohnen.*

Mark Wigley is an architect, author, and dean of Columbia University's Graduate School of Architecture, Planning, and Preservation in New York City. He is the author of *The Architecture of Deconstruction: Derrida's Haunt* (1993) and *White Walls, Designer Dresses: The Fashioning of Modern Architecture* (1995). Wigley cocurated, with Philip Johnson, the groundbreaking MoMA exhibition Deconstructivist Architecture in 1988 and cofounded, with Rem Koolhaas and Ole Bouman, *Volume* magazine in 2005.

Book Review
Christopher Long

Selected Writings on Architecture, Preservation, and the Built Environment

James Marston Fitch
Edited by Martica Sawain
New York and London: W. W. Norton, 2006

Architekturgeschichte und kulturelles Erbe—Aspekte der Baudenkmalpflege in Ostmitteleuropa

Edited by Beate Störtkuhl
Frankfurt am Main: Peter Lang, 2006

James Marston Fitch is remembered today as one of the founding fathers of historic preservation in the United States. Over the course of a career extending more than six decades, Fitch became the public face of the American preservation movement and one of its most passionate supporters. After visiting Czechoslovakia in the early 1960s and seeing firsthand the country's extensive government-directed preservation education program, he realized that similar professional training in the field was needed in the United States. With Charles Peterson, founder of the Historic American Buildings Survey (HABS), he established the first formal program of preservation studies at Columbia University in 1964; a little more than a decade later, he founded the Graduate Program in Historic Preservation at the University of Pennsylvania. The young "Fitchians" he trained soon emerged as leaders of the country's developing professional preservation cadre. Fitch was active, too, in preservation practice. He served as the first conservator of New York's Central Park in the mid-1970s, and he was a partner and director of historic preservation in the firm Beyer Blinder Belle. Among the many important preservation projects he worked on were the restoration of Grand Central Station and the Ellis Island National Monument.

Fitch's many writings broadly influenced the shape and direction of American preservation. His 1982 book, *Historic Preservation: Curatorial Management of the Built World,*[1] became the bible of the new movement, and his numerous essays on the subject dealt with nearly every aspect of the field. This new book, *James Marston Fitch: Selected Writings on Architecture, Preservation, and the Built Environment,* which includes twenty-four of his essays edited and intro-

Future Anterior
Volume IV, Number 2
Winter 2007

duced by his wife Martica Sawin, offers a useful and representative sampling of Fitch's writings, covering his thoughts on design, the practice and theory of preservation, and urban planning.

What characterizes Fitch's written work is not only the vivacity and perceptiveness of his insights but his insistence that architecture and preservation must be viewed within a larger social, cultural, and environmental context. Only four of Fitch's writings on preservation are reprinted here, but they convey well his preoccupations and his views.

One of his concerns was that preservation move away from its amateurish and populist roots. Fitch understood the importance of a community-based preservation movement, but he was determined to see the field professionalized. He stressed that the new leaders in the field should be academically trained, and he believed that the universities should assume a prominent role in promoting and practicing preservation. Fitch also advocated closer ties with professionals in other, related disciplines, including art conservation, art history, and archaeology. He was particularly enthusiastic about the rise of the new discipline of preservation technology, which brought together scientists and technicians in the field.

But Fitch's concerns went well beyond the narrow frame of the architectural preservation. In one of the essays reproduced in the book, "The Philosophy of Restoration," he sharply condemns the idea of gentrification—buildings, he writes, "should be restored for their original population and not for a new population which has historically no right to be there in the first place"—and he emphasizes the importance of not disturbing existing cultures "which would not survive dispersion or transplantation to another venue."[2] He also calls upon his fellow professionals in the field not to lose contact with those they serve; he is critical of architects and planners for their "frightening neglect, if not contempt for, the already-built world around them"; and he lauds the notion that preservation can be "the central energizing force" in urban renewal.[3]

All of these issues have become gospel in professional preservation circles, doubtless in some measure because of Fitch's advocacy. Indeed, much of what he writes in these pieces seems unremarkable now. Yet there are surprises. One has to do with his strident environmentalism. When Fitch discusses the "reservoir of energy"[4] in old buildings that is wasted with their demolition, he seems to anticipate discussions that would only come to the fore in the past few years.[5] And for those familiar with American preservation efforts of the 1950s and 1960s, it is notable that Fitch was a very early advocate of a holistic approach to saving the built world. His

"Position Paper on Central Park" (1974) and "Visual Criteria for Historic Building Restoration: Determining Appropriate Repair/Cosmetic Treatments" (1978) are informed by a nuanced and thoughtful attitude, one that sought to balance the competing interests of history and present-day use.

At the same time, some of Fitch's concerns in these essays now seem dated. His worries about the pernicious effects of postmodernism belong to another age, as do his musings about the issue of replicas. In this light, it is interesting that Fitch was not more critical in these writings of early preservation efforts, like Colonial Williamsburg, which fostered their own fictions.

What stands out, too, is Fitch's continuing fealty to functionalism in architecture—even as the modernism of his youth was undergoing serious challenges. Among the most arresting essays in this collection is "Utopia Revisited: The Bauhaus at Dessau Forty Years Later," in which Fitch chronicles his visit to the famed school in 1966. At the time, the Bauhaus buildings, badly damaged by years of neglect and abuse, were undergoing the first of several extensive restorations. Like many young architects who came to maturity in the later 1920s, the Bauhaus represented for Fitch "a radiant symbol of a whole new way of life."[6] Even four decades later, he writes gushingly of its power and purity, and the buildings' demise seemed for him to be a symbol of the collapse of the modernist vision around the world:

> [T]he architecture of the entire world is in crisis and it is substantially the same crisis East and West. Our present troubles are not the result of having followed too closely the Bauhaus doctrine, as a self-styled avant-garde would now have us believe. To the contrary they stem from our having completely abandoned the broad lines of theoretical development the Bauhaus projected.[7]

Fitch understood very well that the "Bauhaus vision" was about more than aesthetics, that social utility was a fundamental element of the new design. "The designer," he insists, "must be socially accountable. And this implies a new kind of education—one that would heal the rift between theory and practice, classroom and shop, designer and artisan." But Fitch seems less aware of the deeper social and political meanings of the Bauhaus legacy. Although he writes of the convulsions of change that followed the collapse of the Weimar Republic, he ascribes almost all of what happened to the rise of Hitler and Stalinism and to innate German tendencies:

> German architecture in the East has experienced another destructive force, design by diktat. The first was Hitler's,

demanding an architectural idiom expressive of that mad
Wagnerian nightmare of blood-thinking and *herrenvolk.*
And this was followed by the Stalinesque *ukase.* . . . Both
of these esthetic codes were enforced with typical Prussian thoroughness. They have left German architecture
quite visibly shaken to its roots. In its current condition of
esthetic disequilibrium, the rediscovery of the Bauhaus is
a fortunate development, for its most impressive quality
today is precisely its equilibrium, its effortless mastery of
the means at its disposal.[8]

Certainly, what took place in Dessau and the rest of Germany was in great part the horrific outcome of political and
social disruption. But Fitch was apparently unaware of—or, at
least, unwilling to acknowledge—the role that modernization
itself, and the discontents it spawned, had in the demise of
the modernist program. Almost from the beginning, there were
vocal and persistent protests about the new building culture,
some of them coming from within the ranks of the modernists
themselves.[9] What Germany and the other nations of East
Central Europe experienced over the past century and half
was a consequence of the profound dislocations wrought by
rapid industrialization and urbanization. Modernist architectural culture, however attractive it may have been for some,
was only one of a number of responses to the dilemmas these
changes brought.

I bring this up not to criticize Fitch, who had an unusually
sensitive understanding of the relationship between architecture and forces that give rise to it (and hardly deserves such
judgment), but because this is an issue that goes to the heart
of the complex legacy of twentieth-century building and has
very real consequences for the preservation movement in the
United States. American preservationists for a very long time
were preoccupied with saving our premodern heritage; it has
been only been in the past two decades that we have begun to
engage the much more thorny issues related to modern buildings. Not only are there new technical difficulties inherent in
this effort, but we also face challenges in how we determine
what to save and how we should interpret what we preserve.
In this light, the recent experience of Germany and the other
countries of East Central Europe may be instructive. Because
they have been faced with myriad and sometimes seemingly
intractable problems, professionals working in the preservation field in the region have been especially attentive to
questions about saving the recent past.

Particularly interesting in this regard is a new book,
*Architekturgeschichte und kulturelles Erbe—Aspekte der Bau-
denkmalpflege in Ostmitteleuropa* (Architectural history and

cultural heritage—Aspects of historic preservation in East Central Europe). Edited by Beate Störtkuhl, who teaches at Carl von Ossietzky University in Oldenburg and works at the German Federal Institute for the Study of German Culture and History in Eastern Europe, the book brings together eleven talks given at a special seminar at the university in the fall and winter term of 2002–3. Störtkuhl sought to present the widest possible look at the problems of historic preservation in the region, inviting scholars from Austria, Germany, Latvia, Romania, Poland, and Slovakia to take part. The result is a set of essays on divergent topics and with quite different foci. But taken together, these pieces offer perhaps the best current discussion of preservation efforts in the region.

Störtkuhl's own essay, which serves as an introduction, examines the history of preservation efforts in Germany and surrounding lands, from the early nineteenth century up to the present day. Though a little less than thirty pages long, it offers a remarkably complete and lucid picture of the preservation movement in the region, its genesis, and subsequent development. Her argument is simple and direct: that preservation there has always been a balancing act between scholarship and science on one hand and ideology on the other. Central to preservation efforts have been the twin issues of nationalism and identity, and these played out not only within Germany but also throughout the entire geographic area. Because so much of this terrain represented contested territory for the various national and ethic groups, the preservation movement took on a political and cultural importance that often far outstripped any historical or other considerations. The political division of the region into "East" and "West" during the Cold War only amplified the role of ideology, and these tensions continue to the present day to impact which buildings are preserved and how they are interpreted.

The other ten essays in the book serve as case studies, demonstrating in detail how national and political ideas have affected the trajectory of preservation work in the various countries. Among the most interesting of these studies is Michał Woźniak's article on the restoration of Marienburg castle. Built between the last quarter of the thirteenth and the beginning of the fifteenth centuries in what is now central Poland, the fortress of Marienburg was the seat of the Teutonic Knights until it passed into Polish control in 1466. The area became part of the Prussian state again after the first partition of Poland in 1772. By the nineteenth century, the vast building complex had deteriorated badly, and beginning in 1882, restoration efforts were begun under Konrad Steinbrecht that lasted until 1922. During the Wilhelmine period, Marienburg was described as "the bastion of the German nation in the

East" and as a "bulwark against the Slavs," and such rhetoric only increased during the Nazi years. More than half of the castle was destroyed in savage fighting during the Soviet advance at the end of World War II. After the war, it returned to Polish hands.

Although the Poles had occupied and used the complex for three hundred years, Marienburg remained for them a potent—and unpleasant—symbol of German expansionism and aggression, and for a time, it was unclear what would happen to it. Poland faced enormous preservation challenges in the war's aftermath, not the least of which was the rebuilding of Warsaw, Gdansk, and other major cities. Yet, remarkably, in the late 1950s, the Polish government under Władysław Gomułka, an outspoken nationalist with vehemently anti-German sentiments, began restoration work on the building complex that has continued to the present day.

Woźniak suggests that the lessons of Marienburg are two-fold. The first has to do with the changing nature of preservation itself. The existing castle buildings demonstrate very well the nineteenth-century "Romantic" approach to historic preservation, which stressed stylistic consistency and some-times-fanciful reconstructions. In recent years, those charged with overseeing the new preservation work have recognized that Steinbrecht's restoration, despite its manifest "falsifications," offers a remarkable document of this era, itself worthy of preservation, and they have made efforts to reveal and conserve evidence of his interventions. But the second, and perhaps more important, lesson has to do with the shift that took place over time in understanding the meanings of the castle. Rather than viewing Marienburg as a symbol of German or Polish identity, he writes, "it has gradually become a monument... not of a one-sided nationalist past" but of a shared history. "Its role now is to demonstrate to the public the history the nations, the history of building itself, and the history of preservation."[10]

Such an open and objective approach is undoubtedly key to interpreting the built environment in an age of cultural pluralism and globalization. This idea is repeated in several of the book's other essays, including Hanna Derer's essay on the history of preservation in Romania, Ulrich Schaaf's piece on the changing understanding of the "peace churches" in Jauer/Jawor and Schweidnitz/Świdnica, Imants Lancmanis's study of the Palace of Ruhenthal/Rundāle in Latvia, and Kurt Dröge's contribution on the transnational documentation and maintenance of rural vernacular buildings.

Three of the other essays stand out for what they proffer about the preservation of modern architecture. Milos Kruml and Norbert Templ make impassioned pleas not only for saving isolated works from the "industrial era" but also for preserving the industrial cityscape and its culture. It is not enough, they charge, to protect a few vestigial remains of the machine age: the changes wrought by industrialization altered fundamentally the image and composition of most cities in East Central Europe. To remove those traces or to "historicize" the cityscapes by attempting to return them to something resembling their premodern guises is to deny their very historicity. When one considers the urban renewal projects that have sought to reshape Detroit, Cleveland, Pittsburgh, and other industrial cities in the United States, this plea takes on special force.

The most compelling of the essays, however, is by Slovak historian Dušan Buran, who offers a cautionary tale concerning the Slovak Nationalgalerie in Bratislava. Founded in 1948, the museum was housed in what remained of the so-called Wasserkaserne, a Baroque military barracks, in the old city. Originally, the building had been arranged in a rough square, with a large courtyard in the center. One of its four wings faced the Danube, but this portion of the building had been removed in 1940. When the building complex was converted into the museum, the remaining three wings underwent a thorough conservation. By the mid-1960s, discussions were underway to reconstruct the missing section and house within in it a movie theater, administrative offices, exhibition spaces, a large storage area, and a public library. In 1979, after a lengthy planning and design process (interrupted by the Soviet invasion of Czechoslovakia in the spring of 1968), the building was completed. The new wing, designed by Czech architect Vladimír Dedeček, was in a late-modern "Brutalist-inspired" style, and, almost immediately, it came under criticism. Many considered it sharply out of character with the rest of the old city—a veritable "thorn in the eye." After the Velvet Revolution in 1989, the voices of disapproval only became louder. Some prominent leaders and most of the city's newspapers called for the "monster" to be torn down and replaced either by a replica of the original Baroque structure or by a green space along the river framed by the building's other three surviving wings.[11]

Buran's analysis of the story is both insightful and sharply drawn. He points out that dissatisfaction with the new building is not solely attributable to its modern cast; it has also become a symbol for much of the "totalitarian architecture" found throughout the former Eastern Bloc, one of numerous targets of those who are seeking to eradicate the traces of an unhappy past. But more than that, it is one of the most visible reminders of what many regard as the city's "destruction" during the Communist era. Bratislava was the site of some of the most complete (and generally, unsuccessful) urban rebuilding that took place in the former Czechoslovakia. Much of the inner city was transformed during the 1960s, 1970s, and 1980s: numerous older structures were removed; a freeway was constructed through the heart of the city; and the old palace, which dominates the Bratislava's skyline, was "modernized."

Buran is careful to point out that the questions surrounding the "new wing" of the Nationalgalerie are not as simple as a matter of "old versus new." One might argue, he writes, that the structure should be preserved precisely because it is a symbol of Slovakia's Communist era. He cites the architectural historian Dana Bořutová, who remarked during a roundtable discussion about the building's future: "Far more a symbol of Socialism than this building are its victims"—those buildings that either were not built because of the repression, or that were altered to suit "official taste." But the controversy, of course, also extends beyond politics: it is also matter of aesthetic taste. Buran is quick to point out that a number of important museum buildings constructed in the West in the same period—for example, Marcel Breuer's Whitney Museum in New York City (1966)—represented a "relatively aggressive sculptural architecture," and did not immediately find public favor.[12]

Buran sees the hostility toward the new wing as part of a larger movement, extending back to the 1930s, of opposition toward the city's modernization. The reaction, which has taken place over the last decade, has led to the erection in the old town of a large number of "historicized new structures" in an effort to make the area more "tourist friendly." The net result, aside from flooding the city with "nostalgic kitsch," has been to threaten the very basis of historic preservation, posing questions about what is "real" and what should actually be saved.[13]

This issue is all the more difficult to address if one considers what Fitch describes in one of his essays in *Selected Writings* as the "psychic disorientation"[14] of displaced populations. At the time, Fitch was writing about what he called "physical displacement"—of actually relocating people. But the concept might be readily broadened to encompass social, political, cultural, and temporal displacement. What happened in Bratislava involved all of these forms of disorientation; it is small wonder that many have sought solace in nostalgia, however misplaced.

The situation is little different in most American cities. In preserving the recent past, we will have to confront the same very difficult choices.

Author Biography

Christopher Long, PhD, teaches architectural history and theory in the School of Architecture at the University of Texas at Austin. He is currently serving as director of the school's architectural history program. His work focuses on the history of architecture and design in Central and Eastern Europe, but he also writes about the broader history of architecture and historic preservation. He is the author of *Josef Frank: Life and Work* (2002) and *Paul T. Frankl and Modern American Design* (2007) and is currently working on a book on Adolf Loos's Haus am Michaelerplatz in Vienna (1909–11).

Endnotes

I would like to thank my colleagues in the School of Architecture at the University of Texas at Austin, Michael Holleran, Frances Gale, and Monica Penick, for their thoughtful and incisive comments.

[1] James Marston Fitch, *Curatorial Management of the Built World* (New York: McGraw-Hill, 1982.

[2] Fitch, *Selected Writings,* 176.

[3] Ibid., 178.

[4] Ibid.

[5] During the first energy crisis of the early 1970s, there was a burst of research on "embodied energy" in extant buildings, but the interest in the subject waned during the following decade and has only been revived in recent years.

[6] Ibid., 149.

[7] Ibid., 155.

[8] Ibid., 154.

[9] Throughout the 1920s and 1930s there were ongoing—and sometimes strident— disagreements about the nature of modernism and its meaning. These debates not only reflected the marked divisions within the ranks of the architectural profession, but they presaged the coming debate about modern architecture in the 1950s and 1960s. At the 1930 meeting of the German Werkund in Vienna, for example, a number of the delegates, including Josef Frank and Peter Meyer, publicly criticized Walter Gropius, Mies van der Rohe, and other "radicals" within the Modern Movement, touching off a furious dispute that lasted for months and that would eventually tear the organization apart. See, for example, Joan Campbell, *The German Werkbund: The Politics of Reform in the Applied Arts* (Princeton, N.J.: Princeton University Press, 1978): 206–42.

[10] Störtkuhl, *Architekturgeschicte und Kulturelles Erbe,* 124. All translations from German original by the author.

[11] Ibid., 166–69.

[12] Ibid., 166–72.

[13] Ibid., 173–75.

[14] Ibid., 176.

Call for Submissions

Future Anterior approaches the field of historic preservation from a position of critical inquiry. A comparatively recent field of professional study, preservation often escapes direct academic challenges of its motives, goals, forms of practice, and results. *Future Anterior* seeks contributions that ask these difficult questions from philosophical, theoretical, and practical perspectives. We welcome articles on all topics relevant to historic preservation.

Articles submitted for peer review should be no more than 4000 words, with up to five illustrations. Text must be formatted in accordance with the *Chicago Manual of Style,* 15th Edition. All articles must be submitted in English, and spelling should follow American convention. All submissions must be submitted electronically, on a CD or disk, accompanied by hard copies of text and images. Text should be saved as Microsoft Word or RTF format, while accompanying images should be sent as TIFF files with a resolution of at least 300dpi at 8" by 9" print size. Figures should be numbered clearly in the text. Image captions and credits must be included with submissions. It is the responsibility of the author to secure permissions for image use and pay any reproduction fees. A brief author bio (around 100 words) must accompany the text.

Future Anterior also welcomes shorter articles of less than 2500 words and five illustrations for consideration outside of the peer review process. The same submission requirements apply to these articles.

Acceptance or rejection of submissions is at the discretion of the editorial staff. Please do not send original materials, as submissions will not be returned.

Please mail all submissions to:
Future Anterior
400 Avery Hall
Graduate Program in Historic Preservation
Columbia University New York, NY 10027

Questions about submissions or published articles can be mailed to the above address or to:
futureanterior@columbia.edu

www.arch.columbia.edu/futureanterior

Future Anterior
Volume IV, Number 2
Winter 2007

Future Anterior is a member of FAST-IP
(Federation of Architectural Studies Independent Publications)
www.fast-ip.org

Other member journals include:
Thresholds (http://architecture.mit.edu/thresholds)
Springerin (www.springerin.at/en)
Revista de Arquitectura (www.unav.es/arquitectura)

Ra
REVISTA DE ARQUITECTURA

Ra, *Revista de Arquitectura*, is published yearly by the School of Architecture of the University of Navarra. **Ra** is a forum for results of the academic debate regarding the diverse dimensions of architecture and the city, considering both as cultural realities of unarguable importance and impact, and as objects of careful attention, study and investigation.

Ra aims to specifically assemblage the intellectual production of Theory and History, Urban Planning and Architectural Design Departments, although it is initially open to articles and collaborations from independent professionals and other academic institutions. **Ra** also seeks to feed the perception of architecture as a cultural discipline in the extensive sense of the word.

Articles are published in Spanish and English after a journal selection process conducted by the International Editorial Board. Submissions for the next issue (**Ra** 10) must be received no later than March, 2008.

FOR MORE INFORMATION CONTACT:
Jorge Tárrago Mingo
Coordinator *Ra*
ETS de Arquitectura
Universidad de Navarra
31080 Pamplona. Spain
jtarrago@unav.es

Subscriptions: spetsa@unav.es
http://www.unav.es/arquitectura/publicaciones/pedidos/

Become a *Future Anterior* Sponsor

Future Anterior is a not-for-profit, all-volunteer journal. It is funded by grants and sold at cost in the spirit of making knowledge available to everyone. Donations are critical to helping us accomplish this mission. If you would like to become a sponsor, please fill out this page and mail it—with a check payable to "Columbia University"—to:

Future Anterior
Historic Preservation Program
Graduate School of Architecture, Planning and Preservation
400 Avery Hall
1172 Amsterdam Avenue
Columbia University
New York, NY 10027

All sponsors will be recognized in each issue of *Future Anterior* and receive a one year subscription to the journal.

Please check appropriate sponsorship level:

Individual Sponsor: ❏ begins at $100/year
Institutional Sponsor: ❏ begins at $500/year
Patron: ❏ begins at $1000/year

Name*
_____

Address
_____

_____

City
_____

State _____ Zip _____

Country
_____

Institution/Office
_____

_____

_____

Email
_____

*Please provide your name exactly as you would like it to appear in print